# PERPLEXITIES

ALSO BY MAX BLACK:

The Nature of Mathematics
Critical Thinking
Language and Philosophy
Problems of Analysis
Models and Metaphors
A Companion to Wittgenstein's *Tractatus*
The Labyrinth of Language
Margins of Precision
Caveats and Critiques
The Prevalence of Humbug and Other Essays

# MAX BLACK

## PERPLEXITIES

*Rational Choice, the Prisoner's Dilemma, Metaphor, Poetic Ambiguity, and Other Puzzles*

Cornell University Press

Ithaca and London

Copyright © 1990 by Cornell University

All rights reserved. Except for brief quotations in a review, this book, or parts thereof, must not be reproduced in any form without permission in writing from the publisher. For information, address Cornell University Press, 124 Roberts Place, Ithaca, New York 14850.

First published 1990 by Cornell University Press.

International Standard Book Number 0-8014-2230-2
Library of Congress Catalog Card Number 89-34777
Printed in the United States of America
*Librarians: Library of Congress cataloging information appears on the last page of the book.*

*The paper in this book is acid-free and meets the guidelines for permanence and durability of the Committee on Production Guidelines for Book Longevity of the Council on Library Resources.*

*To my great-grandchildren*
*Daniel and Zachary*

# Contents

*Introduction: The Articulation of Concepts*     1

**MEANING AND VERIFICATION**

1    *Some Puzzles about Meaning*     13
2    *Verificationism Revisited: A Conversation*     30

**METAPHOR**

3    *More about Metaphor*     47
4    *How Metaphors Work: A Reply to Donald Davidson*     77

**RATIONALITY**

5    *Ambiguities of Rationality*     95
6    *The "Prisoner's Dilemma" and the Limits of Rationality*     112

**CHOICE THEORY**

7    *Making Intelligent Choices: How Useful Is Decision Theory?*     133
8    *Some Questions about Bayesian Decision Theory*     152

*Contents*

**APPLICATIONS**

| | | |
|---|---|---:|
| 9 | *On Demystifying Space* | 165 |
| 10 | *The Radical Ambiguity of a Poem* | 174 |
| | **Index** | 197 |

# *Publisher's Note*

Max Black was in the process of completing the final editing of the manuscript for this volume when he died on August 27, 1988. He was solely responsible for the selection of the essays and for the order in which they appear in the book, but he was unable before his death to draft a preface.

The Press thanks Jack Kaminsky for seeing the book through to publication. Professor Kaminsky, Black's literary executor and long-time friend, has been unfailingly helpful and generous with his time and efforts. For permission to reprint, thanks are due the editors of the journals and volumes in which the essays originally appeared. (Information on the provenances and dates of publication of the essays may be found at the openings of essays.) The Press is also grateful for the efforts of Victoria Kamsler and Joyce Paleen, who assisted the author in readying the book for publication.

He knew what's what
and that's as high
as metaphysic wit can fly.
                —Hudibras

# PERPLEXITIES

# Introduction:
# The Articulation of Concepts

An alternative title might have been "glimpses of one man's way of doing philosophy." Conscious of the near-absurdity of trying to look over one's own shoulder, I offer these backward glances to encourage beginners and to entertain fellow-practitioners.

## Influences

I became permanently addicted to philosophical investigation as a young Cambridge mathematician, on the verge of a research career, well trained in the natural sciences and the humanities, but oblivious of the very existence of philosophy. I was extraordinarily fortunate to be able to attend the classes of G. E. Moore, at the height of his formidable powers; of Wittgenstein, recently returned to philosophical investigation; and of F. P. Ramsey, whose sudden death was a tragedy for British philosophy. I loved the ferocious but unmalicious disputes of the Moral Sciences Club. These philosophers and their friends influenced me by their dedication as much as by their doctrines. I take this chance to record my gratitude for Susan Stebbing, whose example showed me how a philosophical outlook could support an admirable way of life.

Meanwhile, by joining W. Empson, J. Bronowski, and other

*Introduction*

literary friends in founding the short-lived magazine *Experiment*, I came to profit from the stimulation and encouragement of C. K. Ogden and I. A. Richards. The former accepted for publication my first book on the nature of mathematics when only its title existed; the second aroused my lasting interest in metaphor and other nonscientific uses of language.[1]

A list of others who have influenced me, often through stimulating disagreement, would include Russell, Frege, Hilbert, Brouwer, Carnap, Keynes, Ryle, Brentano, Peirce, and William James. To avoid invidious comparisons I omit names of living contemporaries.

When I became a professor of philosophy, after a decade of teaching mathematics to children and their prospective teachers, I found I needed to learn as much as I could about a wide variety of disciplines, ranging from linguistics and literary criticism to psychology, sociology, and, in recent years, economics. Only at Cornell University could I have found so many conversable colleagues, willing to relieve my ignorance and to engage in extended cooperative investigation.[2]

Thus I became an autodidact by necessity and a rover by inclination, happy to spend so much of my time in learning by teaching—and actually getting paid for it.

Topics

My published writings might be roughly classified with considerable overlaps as expository, critical, and constructive. The first class would include such "popular" books as *Critical Thinking*,[3] which started a new fashion in logic texts, and *The Labyrinth of Language*.[4] The *Companion to Wittgenstein's "Tractatus,"*[5] a decade in preparation, and several later essays in which I partially

---

1. See especially my *Models and Metaphors: Studies in Language and Philosophy* (Ithaca, N.Y., 1962); "More about Metaphor," pp. 47–76 in this volume; and "How Metaphors Work: A Reply to Donald Davidson," pp. 77–91 in this volume.

2. For one influential outcome, see my *Social Theories of Talcott Parsons* (Englewood Cliffs, N.J., 1961).

3. *Critical Thinking*, 2d ed. rev. (Englewood Cliffs, N.J., 1951).

4. *The Labyrinth of Language* (New York, 1968).

5. *A Companion to Wittgenstein's "Tractatus"* (Ithaca, N.Y., 1964).

discharged my great debt to Wittgenstein's provocations, are both expository and critical. The second class would contain many critical essays, such as those on various philosophers of language in *Language and Philosophy*[6] and essays on special topics, such as those on Carnap's semantics,[7] P. Grice on speaker's meaning,[8] J. Austin on performatives,[9] and N. Goodman on symbol systems;[10] also some enjoyable polemics against such influential heresiarchs as Count Alfred Korzybski[11] and B. F. Skinner.[12] The third class has many members, of which I would single out especially my work on "vagueness,"[13] on models and metaphors,[14] on induction and probability,[15] and on rationality.[16]

6. *Language and Philosophy: Studies in Method* (Ithaca, N.Y., 1949).
7. "Logic and Semantics," in *Philosophical Studies: Essays in Memory of L. Susan Stebbing*, ed. A. H. Hannay (London, 1948), reprinted as "Carnap on Logic and Semantics" in my *Problems of Analysis: Philosophical Essays* (Ithaca, N.Y., 1954).
8. "Meaning and Intention: An Examination of Grice's Views," *New Literary History* 4 (1973), pp. 257–79, reprinted in my *Caveats and Critiques: Philosophical Essays in Language, Logic, and Art* (Ithaca, N.Y., 1975).
9. "Austin on Performatives," *Philosophy* 38 (1963), pp. 217–26, reprinted in my *Margins of Precision: Essays in Logic and Language* (Ithaca, N.Y., 1970).
10. "The Structure of Symbol Systems," *Linguistic Inquiry* 11 (1971), pp. 515–38, reprinted in my *Caveats and Critiques*.
11. *Language and Philosophy*, ch. 10.
12. *Caveats and Critiques*, ch. 11.
13. "Vagueness—An Exercise in Logical Analysis," *Philosophy of Science* 4 (1939), pp. 427–55, reprinted in *Language and Philosophy*; and "Reasoning with Loose Concepts," *Dialogue* 2:1 (1963), pp. 1–12, reprinted in my *Margins of Precision*.
14. *Models and Metaphors*.
15. "The Justification of Induction," in *Proceedings of the Tenth International Congress of Philosophy*, Amsterdam, 1949, pp. 791–93; "Self-Supporting Inductive Arguments," *Journal of Philosophy* 55 (1958), pp. 718–25, reprinted in *Models and Metaphors*; "Induction and Probability," in *Philosophy in the Mid-Century*, ed. R. Klibansky (Florence, 1958), 1:154–63; "Can Induction Be Vindicated?" *Philosophical Studies* 10 (1959), pp. 5–16, reprinted in *Models and Metaphors*; "The Raison d'Être of Inductive Argument," *British Journal for Philosophy of Science* 17 (1966), pp. 177–204, reprinted in *Margins of Precision*; "Induction and Probability," in *Contemporary Philosophy: A Survey*, ed. R. Klibansky (Florence, 1968), 2:54–63; "Some Half-Baked Thoughts about Induction," in *Philosophy, Science, and Method*, ed. S. Morgenbesser, P. Suppes, and M. G. White (New York, 1969), pp. 144–49, reprinted in *Margins of Precision*; "Induction and Experience," in *Experience and Theory*, ed. L. Foster and J. W. Swanson (Amherst, Mass., 1970), pp. 135–60, reprinted in *Caveats and Critiques*.
16. "Rationality and Cultural Relativism," in *Problems of Choice and Decision*, ed. M. Black (Ithaca, N.Y., 1975), pp. 128–60; "Some Remarks about Ra-

Introduction

## Starting from Ordinary Language

In trying to solve an engrossing problem, often provoked by some skeptical argument for conclusions offensive to common sense,[17] I have been opportunistic, willing to try anything, from formal argument to the invention of counterexamples and, more ambitiously, the generation of novel concepts. In so doing, I have been distressed, like many other philosophers,[18] by the absence of agreed definitions for slippery vernacular terms. I have therefore repeatedly tried to discover what we mean or should mean by some word in common use. Thus, in continuing studies of rationality, I have been interested in the way literate English speakers use "reason," "reasonable," "justification," "irrational," and their kindred terms. In Austin's happy phrase, I have treated ordinary language as the "begin-all" but emphatically not the "end-all" of what I now prefer to call the *articulation* of concepts. The label is intended to stress the need to synthesize as well as to analyze, and also to recognize the reciprocal influences of parts and wholes. This approach differs from the lexicographer's by ignoring the idiosyncrasies of any particular language and by being ultimately concerned in its own fashion with traditional philosophical problems of ontology, epistemology, and methodology.

My justification for this often despised "traffic with words" can be summarized by the following contentions: (1) Although meaningful words are obviously not themselves concepts, the words we use in thinking provide tangible and manageable starting points for conceptual inquiry. (2) Key words in the philosophical lexicon are borrowed from ordinary language. (3) While articulation is not a novel procedure, having been often used by past masters, contemporary practitioners can now greatly profit from

---

tionality," *Philosophic Exchange* 2 (1977), pp. 65–74; "The 'Prisoner's Dilemma' and the Limits of Rationality," pp. 112–30 in this volume; "The Rationality of Voting," in *Reason, Action, and Experience*, ed. H. Kohlenberg (Hamburg, 1979), pp. 61–70, reprinted in my book *The Prevalence of Humbug and Other Essays* (Ithaca, N.Y., 1983).

17. See, for instance, my struggles with Zeno's paradoxes in *Problems of Analysis*, pt. 2.

18. See Socrates in the *Phaedrus* or G. E. Moore's famous opening of his *Principia*.

the sophisticated products of modern linguistic theory. (4) Such favored alternatives as introspection or *Wesensschau* have a poor track record; practitioners of conceptual articulation can reasonably hope to do better, and have indeed scored rather well by the pragmatic test of results achieved. On the whole, objecting in this connection to "appeal to *words*" seems to me as pointless as reproaching a painter for using brush strokes.

Procedures

In trying to articulate a particular concept, say that of a "cause,"[19] I like to start with an uncomplicated and uncontroversial case of correct use of the corresponding word or expression—a clear case of application "if anything is"—paying special attention to the verbal and nonverbal contexts of utterance. One can usually find a variety of such *paradigm cases*, that is, actual or imagined situations in which the targeted word is indisputably and correctly applied. The subsequent articulative procedure is inductive, proceeding from particular instances to guarded generalizations and integrative grasp.

I differ from some other conceptual analysts in preferring familiar and banal instances of use to ingeniously bizarre ones. So I avoid fantastic, empirically impossible situations, though not neglecting imaginary and improbable but yet empirically possible ones. Currently popular fables about live brains in storage or malicious scientist-demiurges belong in my opinion to the dubious genre of philosophy-fiction.[20]

Further Steps

Description of paradigm cases serves as a prelude to identification of the relevant use-governing *criteria*, and so eventually to exhibition of the encompassing subsystem of semantically and

---

19. See "Making Something Happen," in *Determinism and Freedom*, ed. S. Hook (New York, 1958), pp. 15–30, reprinted in *Models and Metaphors*.

20. Cf. my efforts to bring "Newcomb's Problem" down to earth in *Prevalence of Humbug*, ch. 8.

*Introduction*

pragmatically related words. If all goes well, systematic consideration of the synonyms, antonyms, and paronyms of a targeted concept name ultimately reveals its position in the relevant linguistic field.

It would be unsatisfactory to scrutinize the "deep" conceptual grammar of the enfolding language (*langue*) while neglecting the implicit under-meanings and between-meanings of successful speech (*parole*); the pioneering forays of Austin on "speech acts" and Grice on "conversational implication" leave a vast territory still to be explored. Thorough study of the "pragmatic" aspects of communication would require careful attention to nonverbal "paralinguistic" signs and gestures; a general theory of signs, so promisingly initiated by Peirce, is too important to be left to the swarms of enthusiastic but often naive contemporary "semioticians."[21]

Respecting Common Sense

Conceptual articulation takes for granted much common knowledge. Thus, in describing paradigm cases of perplexity about the reasons, if any, why anybody should be rational,[22] I presuppose much nonesoteric knowledge, shared by author and reader, about the existence and observable behavior of speakers, together with such subjective phenomena as their motivations, and the reasons they offer; also the very existence of the language in question—and much else that is too familiar for a nonprofessional to question.

The present sketch would therefore be seriously incomplete if I did not declare my respect for the "common sense" thus involved. In joining the good company of Thomas Reid and G. E. Moore (in his famous *Defense*), I am perhaps more conscious than

---

21. I hope these remarks may lead a reader to examine such examples of the recommended procedures as can be found in my essays "Making Something Happen," in *Models and Metaphors*, ch. 8; "Explanations of Meaning," in *Models and Metaphors*, ch. 2; and "Reasonableness," in *Prevalence of Humbug*, ch. 2. The case for conceptual articulation will ultimately rest upon its contributions to clarity and insight.

22. Cf. "Why Should I Be Rational?" in *Prevalence of Humbug*, ch. 1.

they were of the difficulty of distinguishing common-sense knowledge derived from one's own direct experience[23] from such indirectly acquired and often vulnerable convictions as that the world is round, or that it has existed for a long time in the past (to take one of Moore's examples). It should be obvious, however, that the most recondite findings of science, expressed in terms remote from those of the language of nonspecialists, still rest upon what might be called *"primitive common knowledge."*

One overriding reason for trusting common sense rather than the disturbing objections of skeptical philosophers is the (commonsensical!) consideration that the former is likelier to be right than the latter. Active philosophers divide into two camps: those who have the courage of their proofs to the point of advising common sense—in C. D. Broad's famous phrase, "to hang itself like Judas Iscariot"—and those who, like myself, let respect for common sense prevail against the extravagant consistency of philosophers who are willing, for instance, to assert the impossibility of communicating even the sense of their own skeptical claims.[24]

In Pursuit of Good Reasons

Despising dogmatism and mystification, I have doggedly searched for sound arguments in support of interestingly contentious conclusions, while becoming increasingly skeptical about the prospects of success, where so many have failed.

The disconcerting prevalence of hidden fallacy even in the works of past masters may partly explain the resurgence of such famous but shaky arguments as the Ontological Proof of God's Existence. A deeper reason may well be the insidious practice of using such ordinary-language words as "knowledge," "perception," "meaning," or "reason" in indefensibly modified technical senses. (I call this practice *distortio*.)

Present-day efforts to replace informal and truncated philosophical arguments (enthymemes) by formal arguments in the

23. Cf. my essay "Scientific Objectivity," in *Prevalence of Humbug*, ch. 3.
24. Cf. my "Linguistic Method in Philosophy," in *Critical Thinking* (Englewood Cliffs, N.J., 1951), ch. 1.

*Introduction*

style of mathematical proofs do not reach the sources of argumentative failure. For a powerful force behind philosophical reasoning is what I have elsewhere called an "archetype," defined as "a systematic repertoire of ideas by means of which a given thinker describes, by *analogical extension,* some domain to which those ideas do not immediately and literally apply."[25]

I now think of archetypes as generating conceptual maps that express imperfectly integrated cognitive structures of interacting wholes and parts. Here, too, much work remains to be done.

Retrospect

On the whole I see my work as having been marked by concern for reasonableness, restrained by a conviction that rationality is not enough; commitment to common sense of a kind that does not shy away from science and philosophy; appreciation and distrust of abstract models; as much interest in the unformulated stratagems and implicit understandings of speech as in the normative codes of grammar and logic.

Though no enemy of theory, I have always been interested, like a poet, in minute particulars. Striving to live in "uncertainty, mysteries, doubt, without any irritable reaching after fact and reason" (Keats), is occasionally rewarded by calm and exhilarated contemplation: it is a well-kept secret that philosophical investigation, like music, can be enjoyable. I have sought to make my own "way of life" one that embraces humaneness and rejects humbug, with emphasis on "fellow feeling" and respect for the integrity of other human beings: my moral position can be crystallized in the defeasible maxim "Do no harm."

Never having belonged to any philosophical school, I dislike the label of "ordinary language philosopher"; but I would settle for logician, "detached empiricist" (J. Passmore), and active skeptic (in the spirit of Goethe's *tätige Skepsis*).

Those who expect philosophers to provide an inspiring *Weltanschauung*, based on armchair definitions of what is "really

25. *Models and Metaphors*, p. 241.

real," may find my brand of conceptual clarification disappointingly unambitious; I have never found it so or thought time spent in combating muddle and confusion wasted. Unlike "neopositivists," I have no principled objections to ontology. Yet I wonder how biology would look today if its founders had insisted on a priori investigations of "the nature of life" instead of starting from meticulous observations of animal behavior. Let those who hope to do better than Spinoza keep on trying; I shall be content meanwhile with the more modest, though arduous, task of casting some light in dark places.

# MEANING AND VERIFICATION

# I

## Some Puzzles about Meaning

The basic question which I would like to raise is, What is meaning? Or, if you prefer it, What are meanings? in the plural. Or, to put it somewhat more pompously, I should like to become clearer about the nature of meaning.

This way of stating the problem implies that I am somewhat muddled about the subject, which is certainly the case. On the other hand, I am in excellent company, since many thinkers of the highest ability, with Aristotle at their head, have tried unsuccessfully to answer the question. It is rather extraordinary that their answers should be so varied and, indeed, mutually incompatible. So we can be sure of one thing, that nearly all of them are wrong. Probably, at most one of them is close to the truth, and the chances are, on general principles, that none of them is. On the other hand, the question itself is obviously of prime practical, as well as theoretical, importance. We are constantly faced, in private life and in public affairs, with questions of the form, What does he mean? What does he really mean? What are we to make of that statement? and so on. Sometimes one's very survival depends upon a good answer. One could cite many anecdotes to illustrate this: We have all heard of the famous Charge of the Light Brigade. That extraordinary episode resulted from a misin-

Reprinted, by permission of Lawrence Erlbaum Associates, from *Human Communication: Theoretical Explorations,* ed. A. Silverstein (New York: Wiley, 1974), pp. 81–93.

*Meaning and Verification*

terpretation of a message: a simple direction was misunderstood, and so the famous Light Brigade thought they had to charge at the guns and went to their deaths.

In New York not long ago, I saw a sign that read, "The No-Embarrassment Barber Shop," and to this day I don't know what that meant. I need not supply further examples. It is clear that problems of interpretation, of grasping meaning, constantly arise. Furthermore, our skill in handling these tasks will be influenced, for better or worse, by the theories, whether elaborate or rudimentary, that we have at the back of our minds.

One embarrassment is that no good theory is available; and behind that is the more disturbing fact that we lack a good methodology, so that nobody really knows how to look for the answer.

Let us begin with some elementary reflections about the type of question that we are asking. The question, I remind you, is the deceptively simple one, What is meaning?

Let us take, by way of analogy, the question, What is electricity? Now there you might suppose that answers are readily available—and indeed they are; one learns in elementary courses in physics, or from a textbook, just what electricity is. But a philosopher, or indeed an inquisitive child, may not be satisfied with those answers. You might tell a child the kind of thing that you find in a good textbook of electricity, and at the end of it the child might reasonably say, "Well, I know what electricity does—it lights lamps and gives you shocks and so on—but what really *does* all this? What is this thing called electricity, which is responsible for all of those effects?" The point here is that this is no longer a scientific question. A scientist is satisfied when he can tell you what electricity does. If you now raise questions of the form, Well, is it a sort of spirit? Is it perhaps a kind of fluid? Is it a substance? or Is it perhaps just a fiction, invented only to make phenomena easier to describe? these questions, whether you regard them as legitimate or not, are not, strictly speaking, scientific. They are typically philosophical questions. For something which, from a certain standpoint, is perfectly familiar, has, from another perspective, become mysterious.

One possible definition of a philosopher might well be that he is somebody who is apt to find the familiar mysterious. There is a peculiar kind of philosophical puzzlement which arises when something with which we are quite familiar suddenly appears not only mysterious but in a certain sense inconceivable.

To take an example close to our topic: There is nothing extraordinary about talking to somebody else and understanding what is being said. But if you have the idea, which is natural enough, that the other person's thoughts and feelings are impenetrably hidden from you, that he is somewhere—how shall we say it—inside his body, or behind his face, then the idea of the gap between yourself and him can, from a philosophical point of view, seem extraordinarily strange and mysterious. How is it possible that another mind, which manifests itself to me only as an appearance, should be able to be in communication with me?

Take another example: We are accustomed to making statements about the future, and I can say with reasonable confidence that I shall be leaving Rhode Island tomorrow. But—the future does not exist yet; and some people even think that it is not yet determined. How can I, here and now, make true statements about the future, when there is this logical gap between now and what is yet to come?

Those of you who have taken philosophical courses will be familiar with this kind of point; anybody to whom such trains of thought seem perverse is, perhaps happily, immune from philosophical wonder and puzzlement. But the existence of philosophical perplexity is a fact; that nearly all people at a certain age suffer from it is another fact; and that some people never recover is still another. Tolstoy, in one of his autobiographical sketches, says that as a young man he was so caught up in some of these philosophical perplexities, especially after reading Bishop Berkeley, that at one point he found himself doing the following absurd thing: jumping around very fast, in the hope, perhaps, of finding a void behind him, before he had time to reconstruct it. That, perhaps, verges upon the pathological.

Well, let us now consider what the main philosophical puzzles are in connection with meaning. One that we might mention arises from the extraordinary disparity between certain linguistic means and their nonlinguistic consequences. You may be asked a question in a certain situation, having to choose between the

*Meaning and Verification*

physically trifling sounds "yes" and "no," and a great deal may turn on whether you make the one sound or the other. People have been killed by hearing the word "yes." A man asks whether his son died in the accident; on hearing "yes," he has a stroke and dies. That already looks extraordinary; it seems fantastic that a puff of wind, something which, considered as a physical act, is trivial, should have such massive consequences. And throughout the history of mankind, people have been extraordinarily impressed by what has been called the magic of words. This has been inflated in mythology and religion to the superstition that if you can find the right sound, the right puff of wind, then you can have control over spirits, other men, or nature.

Closely related is the point that very slight differences in the sound can make the difference between the meaningful and the nonsensical. For example, let us take two sounds which are very close: first, the sound of "pin," which you all understand; and, now with a slight change, "pon," which nobody understands. (According to the large Oxford Dictionary, there is no such word in the English language.) It is not a matter of your being ignorant, but of there being a meaning attaching to one sound and not to the other.

Sometimes such slight differences can have monstrous consequences. There was, in the fourth century after the birth of Christ, a famous theological controversy that turned upon the following two Greek words: "homoousian" and "homoiousian," meaning roughly "of the same substance" and "of like substance," respectively. The question at issue was, whether Son was of the same substance as the Father, or simply of an analogous, or like, substance. Many people lost their lives because they chose to say "homoousian" rather than "homoiousian" or vice versa. So much depended upon an insignificant vowel. Or compare the difference, say, between "killing" a person and "calling" him.

How is it possible that such almost imperceptible differences should make all that difference? How is it that certain sounds can be meaningful and others be meaningless when, physically speaking, there seems almost nothing to choose between them?

What is the common-sense answer? In the pin-pon case it

might be that, after all, there are things called "pins" and there are no such things as "pons." I hope you can see at once that this answer, which is one that you might get from a layman, really cannot satisfy us.

In the first place, what does it mean to say that there are things that are called "pins"? Isn't that really a trivial transformation of the original question? If "pins" means what it does mean, then perhaps in the intended sense, there *must* be things called "pins." So, introducing the word "called" does not really help us much. In the second place, we said that there are no things called "pons"; well, how do we know? Perhaps there are. Perhaps there are "pons" around in the world, and we just haven't heard about them. And in the third, but not the last, place, there are many meaningful words and expressions to which no real things correspond. Consider the word "unicorn," or the expression "completely honest President of the United States." These have meaning: a *question* can be raised about the existence of unicorns even by those who don't believe in their existence. So our first formula, that a word has meaning if it stands for things in the world, is unacceptable.

Now, for a moment, let us jump to another kind of case, which may seem a little easier to handle. Consider the case of a personal name—and why don't we take, switching countries, "Pompidou." Of course, here we have a proper name and not a general one, but still the name is somehow or other meaningful. What would common sense say about this? How is it that "Pompideau" (you will notice I have made a slight change in the sound), for all we know, has no meaning? Here again, the common-sense formula, that there is somebody called "Pompidou," seems unsatisfactory because it is unclear what "called" means. No doubt you can find the name in the Paris telephone directory. But that looks inessential. *Must* a man have his name in the telephone directory? You might say, "Well, if you were to meet him and say, 'Pompidou,' he would look at you or reply or do *something*." But how do you know that he wouldn't do the same if you said "Pompideau"? Especially if you were an American.

There seems to be a sort of gap; over here is the sound (the name), and there, at a conceptual distance, is the person. But if that gap is there, how is it that the name "attaches" to the person?

Let us imagine, in the manner of science fiction, that in some other constellation, people have been worried by this philosophical difficulty. So they have decided to eliminate the gap. As soon as a child is born in their world, they simply tattoo a name indelibly onto the skin; and now there is no gap. But now a terrestrial philosopher arrives by rocket and asks the same tiresome question: How do you people understand the connection between the name and the person? They answer, "Look at the tattoo," But then he says, "Why should that name, tattooed on that skin, be *his* name and not some other person's?" There is nothing that guarantees that if I carry a name around, that's my name. Suppose I choose to tattoo "Pompidou" on my skin. Does that make "Pompidou" my name? Or suppose I just say, as I do now, "My name is Pompidou" and repeat that formula with boring frequency. Has it become my name; and if not, why not?

I have been giving you some glimpses, as simply as I can, of how some fundamental questions of philosophical semantics arise. By this time, we should be entitled to suspect that the meaning of a word cannot be some objective correlate—the *bearer* of a proper name, or something less obvious in the case of a general name. Yet the idea that there must be an "objective correlate" that *is* the meaning dies hard. And it can arise in all sorts of connections.

Let me tell you, now, about some of the types of theories that have been proposed. All of these theories, though some may sound rather extraordinary, have been elaborately defended, sometimes for centuries. All have certain advantages and corresponding weaknesses.

In connection with the case of a personal name, it is tempting to suppose that the thing itself—in this case, the man himself—is what is meant. For when I say "Pompidou," if I am using the word correctly, I am trying to refer to that very man.

This has sometimes been called, in the philosophical literature, the "bearer" theory. The basic idea is that the man meant is the bearer of the name and that the meaning of a name is the actual person or thing. There are real, actual things in the world; and, in some way or other yet to be explained, words are attached to, or correlated with, those things, and those very things are the meanings.

This is somewhat paradoxical, but paradox may have to be accepted, no matter what view you take. It would follow, for example, that you can eat meanings. If I point to something and say, I want *that* ice cream, and get it, then when I eat it, I am literally eating the meaning. And by the time I have eaten it up, that meaning has been destroyed, and so I can't talk about it anymore. So that if my wife asks me, "Did you enjoy that ice cream?" I say, "I can't tell you." She retorts, "Why not?" until she realizes that I am talking like a philosopher and shuts up. In general, one of the obvious difficulties of the "bearer" theory, as we have already seen, is that it seems to preclude talking about the nonexistent or the merely possible. But one of the obvious and enormous advantages of language, or of symbolism generally, is that it enables us to talk about what has not happened, but might. Or what did happen, and no longer exists. It is very hard to square a "bearer" theory with the existence of history or with the possibility of prophecy.

A different kind of theory, having a certain formal resemblance, but otherwise very different in character, is that some meaningful items in the vocabulary stand for corresponding abstract entities. For example, if I use a word like "red," then there is something called "redness," and a certain abstract property that can be manifested in any number of places, and the word "red" (or the word "redness") is a name for that abstract entity. You notice that this theory would have to be modified to fit the case of personal names, but even there one could make a case for saying that a person is an abstraction—that what actually *happens* in reality is an instantaneous condition, a time-slice, and when we speak of Pompidou or Nixon, we are speaking of an abstraction. Some of you will know that the General Semanticists have insisted on this, and have said with some plausibility that if you talk about Nixon *in 1958* you must not confuse him with Nixon *in 1973*. So that if you ignore the date, you are employing an abstraction, and a questionable one. A case can be made for saying that persons, as well as institutions, books, theories, are all abstractions and that

## Meaning and Verification

when we use language, we typically talk in terms of abstractions.

The link between the two theories is that they both take names as paradigms of words having meaning. Ryle once invented a quaint label for this kind of theory, namely, "'Fido'-Fido theory" (the name "Fido" conceived as standing for the dog Fido).[1] The "bearer" theory and the abstract entity theory are examples, since in both cases the meaning of the name is thought of as something correlated with the name itself, though in one case you have a nominalistic type of theory with particular, individual things as the meanings, while in the other you have a "realistic" theory.

Other thinkers have thought that any theory of this character suffers from a fatal weakness. The objection is, roughly speaking, that the meaning of terms must reside in human beings, not in objects external to them. Meaning is a human product; there is no natural correlation between the word "Fido" and the dog of that name. If there is a connection, it is something created by human beings. So meaning is located in human intentions or purposes and so, ultimately, in the human mind. This point of view, as old as Aristotle, has been reaffirmed by thousands of philosophers, psychologists, and linguists. We might call it a "mentalistic" type of theory.

One important variety is based on the idea that meaning is a matter of having a distinctive image. A physicalistic variant is based on the idea that there is some lasting pattern or structure, in the brain, or in the central nervous system—anyway, in the body—which *is* the meaning. Some writers have talked of a so-called engram, a sort of trace in the brain supposedly produced by appropriate external stimuli.

The basic idea, then, is that the meaning of any word, say that of any example I have already used, depends upon something about the individual speaker concerned, or about groups of speakers who have similar neurological or psychological structures.

A fine example of this approach can be found in Ferdinand de Saussure's famous book *Course in General Linguistics*,[2] which has exerted so much influence on generations of linguists. There

---

1. G. Ryle, "The Theory of Meaning," in *The Importance of Language*, ed. M. Black (Ithaca, N.Y., 1968).
2. Ferdinand de Saussure, *Course in General Linguistics* (New York, 1959).

you will find a schematic diagram, locating the speaker's meaning in his mind, as the starting point for a process of translation into a physical message and eventual translation back into a corresponding meaning in the hearer's mind. (For present purposes, it does not matter whether the meaning is supposed to be located in a mind or in a brain.) Essentially the same conception is to be found in the writings about language, still well worth reading, of the great philosopher John Locke.[3] This type of view continues to be very popular: there is something about it that strikes the layman as obviously right.

The root idea, then, is that meaning is, roughly speaking, located in the head or in the mind. In communication, we get a transformation of the initial mental or neurological event into a physical process, followed by reception by the hearer and a corresponding de-translation. Whether the hearer understands correctly then depends upon something happening in his mind or brain.

Many years ago I argued publicly with Bertrand Russell about the nature of meaning. He said at the time—but of course he often changed his mind with fantastic rapidity—that every meaningful word had its corresponding mental image. And I said, "So if I now say to you, speaking as fast as I possibly can, 'Almost certainly you're in error,' you think that with every word that I said, each one of which had a meaning that you understood, there was a corresponding image." And he replied, emphatically, "There *has* to be." That's a mark of one kind of serious philosopher. Having found an answer that satisfies him, he will legislate that it *must* be right, no matter what. If you can't notice the images, then, by God, or Something, they must be unconscious or passing too fast for you to observe them. Of course, physiologists will sometimes say the same sort of thing. There must be a process in the brain (what else could it be?), and if we haven't observed these processes, they must be there all the same.

I would like you to see that nothing compels us to accept any such theory. Let us take the image theory first. There is, as all of us know, considerable doubt as to whether imagery is sufficiently

---

3. See John Locke, "Of Words," in *An Essay Concerning Human Understanding*, ed. A. C. Fraser (Oxford, 1894), bk. 3.

prevalent to do the job. My introspective reports are of no interest to anybody who isn't a friend or a relative, and of precious little interest to them; but for what it is worth, I believe that I have very little imagery. As I am talking to you, I can hear the sound of my voice, but that's all. I am not aware of any imagery—and if you insist that I *must* be having unconscious imagery, that's your privilege—for what it is worth.

However, we can bypass this dispute in the following way: Let us assume (what certainly should not be done, except for the sake of argument) that the imagery is there. Let us also concede that there may be a special situation in which somebody produces distinct and articulated imagery when we tell him: "The time is four o'clock."

I might say, in passing, that William James thought that even words like "the" had corresponding images. If you read his *Principles of Psychology*,[4] you will find interesting passages about the imagery which is supposed to go with words like "and," "if," and "but"; he thought there was an "and" feeling, an "if" feeling, and so on. I am going to grant all of this for the sake of argument (though I don't believe it). I cannot conceive what it would be like to have a "the" feeling, but if somebody is going to claim that he has a distinctive image that goes with "the," I will accept his word. Similarly for the other words in our sentence: perhaps "time" induces some kind of flowing feeling. "Is" looks problematic, but let us be generous and assign an image to it as well. And so on. So there was, we suppose, a train of distinctive imagery.

Now, the crucial question is: Supposing that the hearer we have imagined really does have that train of imagery, how does he know what those images mean? Let us suppose, so long as we are being fanciful, that we have some extraordinary device by means of which we can verify the existence of this train of images, even reinduce them in somebody else. So that when I sit in front of this machine, and the operator presses the buttons, I get a train of images just like the images that the hearer had. *Now* do I now know what he meant? Why should I?

4. William James, *Principles of Psychology* (New York, 1950), ch. 9.

Take a more trivial case, say, that of any color word, such as "red." It could happen, by some kind of freakish mechanism, that when you said "red," I always had a green image. Would that mean that I couldn't understand what "red" meant? Well, of course not, since I could always make the appropriate correction. But the fact is, I would not need to make any correction. Whether I have the green image in my head or not has nothing to do with understanding what you say; all that matters is that when I see something which is properly called red, I recognize it and use the right word. What goes on in my mind may be subjectively important but does not determine the semantics of the word. And the same conclusion applies in general. To put it another way, the existence of images simply pushes the whole problem one stage further back, since we are still faced with the problem of explaining what the supposed images mean.

Philosophers from Aristotle to the present have thought that there was some kind of primitive language, *Ursprache*, composed of images and even having a distinctive grammar. But if there is a language of images, then that language itself must have meaning. One might ask for the meaning of the images, and the meaning might be misinterpreted.

You can conceive of a child being taught by somebody who believed this theory, and upon being told, "The time is four o'clock," showing by his actions that he thought it was time for breakfast. But when you check on the imagery (if that even makes sense), you find that the imagery is right—only when the image that we associate with "four o'clock" occurs in the child it means "breakfast," not four o'clock. So you have got essentially the same problem. How does the image mean? By this strategy you move only from something relatively observable, the linguistic phenomenon, to something merely postulated, a mysterious and inaccessible surrogate.

I can make a similar point about the physicalistic theory that identifies meaning with some supposed engram or brain trace. Again, a fantastic hypothesis will help us to understand the issues.

To the best of my knowledge, nobody has ever seen an engram, nor is there any hope, in the foreseeable future, of finding a distinctive neurological structure that corresponds, let us say, to the word "red." But once again, let us take a leap into some fantastic future in which we can directly observe people's brains. So we say "red," while the brain-viewing machine observes the hearer's cerebrum and central nervous system. To make things a little easier for us, let us suppose that the machine shows a particularly active system of neurons arranged in *this* pattern:

# RED

Very convenient!

So somebody says, "Aha! Now, at last, after 2,000 years of inconclusive debate, you can see the meaning: there it is, right there in his brain." Is there anything wrong with that argument? (At this point, somebody will inevitably suggest that "r-e-d" does after all spell "red.") Well, how do we know that "r-e-d" *means* red? There may well be some language—if not, we can invent one—in which "r-e-d" means green.

Or put it this way: suppose we look at his brain, see the r-e-d constellation, and are convinced that he must know the meaning. But in order to check up, we now show him all sorts of color samples with very strong positive and negative inducements to answer sincerely and correctly. Thus if he recognizes the red card, he gets a thousand dollars right away; but if he doesn't, he gets whipped a thousand times. (And he's not a masochist, either.) So we show him the *green* card—he has every inducement, is panting and sweating in his eagerness—and says, "That's red!" A thousand lashes! (And all the time the constellation is glittering in his head.) So what are we going to say? That he *must* understand the word, because the meaning is right in his head? Of course, that's absurd. Any person who still retained some common sense, after being exposed to higher education, would say that if that is what the theory implies, then, so much the worse for the theory. It is perfectly clear that the man who cannot properly discriminate between colors, in cases where he has every inducement to do so, cannot understand the use of the word, and whatever is going on in his brain is irrelevant.

*Some Puzzles about Meaning*

So we pass on, by a natural transition, to theories that identify meaning with behavior. Given the train of thought I have just presented, it is tempting to think that grasp of meaning must, surely, be a matter of what the person *does* and can do. Then, if it should turn out that we also find some supplementary physiological or mental criteria, so much the better. But when we talk about a person's meaning something, what we really have in mind is some kind of behavior.

Well, that sounds promising; but the question is, What behavior? What behavior shows that somebody really understands the word? In the case of color terms, one might think of plausible test situations. You get somebody to discriminate between colors. But please notice that *that* simple test is already somewhat more complicated than it might seem. If I find an unsophisticated person and have a supply of color samples on hand, I still have to *talk* to him in order to get him to take the test. Try doing it without saying anything. Turn up somewhere in the middle of Africa, with a whole lot of color samples, and a word from the local vocabulary—let's suppose it to be "ujgi." Now, in the cause of methodological purity you are not going to talk to these people: you are just going to do this particular experiment, which is to find out whether "ujgi" means "red." What *do* you do? If you merely say "ujgi" while shuffling the color samples, they will probably think you are crazy. It is essential, even for this simple experiment, that the person you are experimenting with understands what you are doing, and understanding presupposes communication, and communication presupposes mastery, via language, of a number of abstract ideas.

Consider a familiar utterance such as "I am trying to get you to sort these colors." Now, if the hearer can understand that, you can perform differential experiments on whether, say, "shocking pink" means anything to him, and if so, what, and so on. This sort of experiment, I want to suggest, has to be conducted against a background that presupposes rather sophisticated linguistic skills. And conversely, where such skills cannot be confidently assumed, as, say, in the case of very young children, the corresponding behavioral tests become almost impossible to perform. Any young parent will testify, without recourse to any recondite observation, that it is hard to know whether a child understands a word, because there is no simple behavioral test.

I should like, finally, to mention one more type of theory which might perhaps be called, somewhat provocatively, the "no meaning" theory.

Stated very crudely, the basic idea of this type of theory is that the question we started from, formulated as, What *is* the meaning of a word, an expression, or a sentence? is already misleading, because it suggests there is something to be looked for. And the various types of theories that I have been sketching all accept that suggestion. Various theorists have identified meaning with the man who bears a name, or some abstract entity to which the label is attached, or part of the mental stream, or neurological traces; and these answers, if they were right, would all presuppose that meaning was something separately identifiable. Now the "no meaning" type of theory attacks that presupposition as a fundamental mistake. Belief that meaning is some kind of entity is, indeed, a special case of a more general mistake, of confusion about what some philosophers call "logical grammar." It is very often the case that presuppositions about what a word refers to are erroneously based on the parallel uses of that word and words of very different kinds of meaning in the same grammatical classes of sentence. Thus "meaning" and "length" are used in very nearly identical linguistic ways and are therefore erroneously assumed to be similar in the logical class of event they refer to.

Many writers have said that the structure of language seems, in some ways, almost deliberately misleading. Take a child and say that a certain place on the map is North Ithaca and another place South Ithaca. If this child is either rather stupid or some sort of precocious philosophical genius, he may say, "Okay, I know where North Ithaca is, and I know where South Ithaca is, but where's *just* Ithaca?" And you reply, "Right here—all of this is Ithaca." But now comes the flash of genius or imbecility: The child insists on knowing also where *"just* North" is. Now, if you should point in the right direction, you might seriously mislead the child, because he might think that just as there is a place here called Ithaca, so up there, somewhere, there is something called North. And if he has that idea, and has any talent for philosophy, he might even tell you that it is very strange that two different

## Some Puzzles about Meaning

places—North and Ithaca—should both be in some mysterious way right *here*. Please notice that the easy way out, of saying "Well, North is only a direction" is no answer at all, because this child, if he really is a prodigy, can say, "Well, what's a direction?" And how are we to answer *that*?

This is a crude and manufactured example of how the structure of ordinary language can confuse thought. There are more impressive examples. I shall mention only one, connected with that fascinating and confusing word, infinity. There are people who think of infinity as if it were some definite place. A talented man who taught me mathematics long ago thought about infinity in that way, and I can still remember a favorite slogan of his, that infinity was "a place where things happen that don't." He would explain his idea in this way (and please remember that he was quite serious): Take a curve that has asymptotes, say, a rectangular hyperbola. Now, if you go up a rising branch in the direction of the $y$-axis, then, of course, you always remain at a distance from that axis: the distance gets smaller and smaller the farther you go up (for that's partly what we mean by the curve being asymptotic); but no matter how far you go, there will always be a gap. But, when you "get to infinity," he suggested, something happens that doesn't; namely, there will be contact. And in fact, this rising branch of the curve will turn up down below, infinitely far down. Because where there's a continuous curve, the crossover happens at infinity, and infinity is down here as well as up there—it's one and the same place. Obviously this talented teacher loved this confusing idea—and you can see how well he taught, because I can still remember that particular lesson. Other people have been known to talk this way about infinity, as if it were some place a very, very long way away. Thus it is sometimes said that parallel lines always stay the same distance apart, until you get to infinity, or more precisely, the point of infinity associated with all those parallel lines, and at infinity they intersect. This case of a confusion in logical grammar can be cleared up by pointing out that infinity is not a place beyond the finite, that the adjective "*infinite*" and the noun "infinity" are used in special ways. (Notice, for example, that we have no noun "finity"—and for good reason.) There is no time, unfortunately, to pursue this further.

*Meaning and Verification*

Now, the basic idea behind the "no meaning" approach is that the term "meaning" functions somewhat like "infinity" in this respect. Put crudely and rather misleadingly, there is no such thing as *the* meaning of a term, or *the* meaning of an expression, or *the* meaning of a sentence. And any search for the meaning is doomed to failure at the start: it is as pointless and self-defeating as the search for some *place* called "infinity." You could scour the universe and you would never find infinity, not for lack of technical skill, but because there is a logical confusion behind the effort. Similarly, the "no meaning" approach claims that there is logical confusion in looking for anything that is the meaning. Please notice that this kind of view by no means implies that the word "meaning" is meaningless, any more than the remarks I made about "infinity" imply that mathematicians or physicists, who talk about infinity, with proper precautions, are talking nonsense. If I say the limit of $1/2^n$ as $n$ goes to infinity is zero, that use of infinity is perfectly respectable. And I can use the mathematical symbol for infinity and understand it, without supposing that there is some number which is denoted by the infinity mark. Similarly, when I say that "nephelococcygian" (a word that is in the dictionary) means, roughly, "cloud-cuckoolandish" or "visionary," I have succeeded *in telling you what it means*. So there is no doubt at all that meaning exists and can be communicated.

Well, what then can the "no meaning" approach say positively? Something of this sort: that the word "meaning" has basically a relational function, expressing a connection *between symbols.* That is the crucial point; it need not be a relation between a word and something nonverbal, but may be regarded as a relation between symbols. I am not suggesting this as the whole story, but this is at least a highly salient feature of the approach. So when I say, "nephelococcygian" means, say, "visionary," I am saying—very roughly, of course—that where you would otherwise have used the word "visionary," now you can say "nephelococcygian" instead. I am therefore offering a sort of equation of synonymy. And this approach can be made to fit, with some stretching, even the so-called ostensive type of case—where I define by pointing to something. If somebody doesn't know what a file folder is, and I say, "That's a file folder," it looks as if I am setting up a connection between the thing itself and something verbal. But it might be held that even here we encounter a kind of synonymy. For the learner must be able to recognize *what* I call a "file folder" by means of some other description. This is controversial, however.

At any rate, this is the general pattern, and you may gather, from the way that I have been talking, that I am more inclined to this relational type of view than to any of the others that I have been discussing. It has all sorts of difficulties but also has a number of inviting possibilities.

I have time only to hint at some of the implications. One is that statements of meaning belong to a sophisticated self-referential level of language. One might get along without the word "meaning" at all, if communication were fairly smooth, which is not always the case. There is a primary level of language where you learn words for people, events, animals, states of mind, and so on. It is only when communication becomes problematic or defective that we need words like "meaning" in order to resolve our difficulties. This is connected with the point I have already made, that in order even to understand a question about meaning, you must already possess many basic linguistic skills. The pattern I am recommending, therefore, looks somewhat like this: There is a basic linguistic level at which we talk about nonverbal things, and there is another, so-called metalinguistic level, at which we use language to talk *about* language. "Meaning" belongs to this "higher" level. Questions about meaning are, roughly speaking, questions about the functioning of language. They are to be answered by showing how parts of the language can replace one another.

What I have just said is all very crude and raises all manner of provoking questions.[5] But that, after all, was my purpose in presenting such a view of meaning.

---

5. One such question that will occur to many readers is that of how one can decide whether what someone has said really means anything or whether it is nonsense. Often, non-sense utterances appear to have meaning because they are cast in a form whose logic is similar to a class of utterances that are meaningful. An example of this class of mistake was presented earlier in this chapter, i.e., the belief that meaning is an entity, arising because the word "meaning" is used in types of sentences which also use nouns that identify entities. A treatment of this important question will be found in my *Labyrinth of Language* (New York, 1969), pp. 105–10, 181–87.

# 2

# Verificationism Revisited: A Conversation

A. When I said that the so-called Principle of Verifiability (*PV*) was dead, you retorted, "But its ghost goes marching on." I have now reviewed, as you suggested, the curious history of the Principle and its progeny.

We agreed, did we not, to think of the original version of the Principle as being expressed by Wittgenstein's remark:[1]

Der Sinn eines Satzes ist die Methode seiner Verifikation.

or in Schlick's English translation:[2]

---

Reprinted, by permission, from *Grazer Philosophische Studien* 16/17 (1982), pp. 35–47.

1. Made in a discussion with Schlick and Waismann, on January 20, 1930; in Friedrich Waismann, *Ludwig Wittgenstein und der Wiener Kreis*, ed. B. F. McGuinness (Oxford, 1967), p. 79. The context was a discussion of Schlick's suggestion that the rules of "logical syntax" might perhaps be empirically established. On December 22, 1929, Wittgenstein said, "[W]enn ich den Sinn des Satzes nie vollständig verifizieren kann, dann kann ich mit dem Satz auch nichts gemeint haben. Dann heißt der Satz auch gar nichts. Um den Sinn eines Satzes festzustellen, müßte ich ein ganz bestimmtes Verfahren kennen, wenn der Satz als verifiziert gelten soll" (ibid., p. 47).

The Principle was brought to public notice in Waismann's paper on the logical analysis of the concept of probability, *Erkenntnis*, I (1930–31). Echoing Wittgenstein, he said, "Eine Aussage beschreibt einen Sachverhalt. Der Sachverhalt besteht oder er besteht nicht. . . . Kann auf keine Weise angegeben werden, wann ein Satz wahr ist, so hat der überhaupt keinen Sinn; denn *der Sinn eines Satzes ist die Methode seiner Verifikation*" (p. 229; emphasis added).

2. "Meaning and Verification," *Philosophical Review* 44 (1936), here quoted from Moritz Schlick, *Gesammelte Aufsätze* (Hildesheim, 1969), p. 340; hereafter cited in text as *GA*.

## Verificationism Revisited: A Conversation

The meaning of a proposition is the method of its verification.

So I shall understand by a *verificationist* anybody willing to affirm *The Dictum* (in either its German or English formulation).

B. What struck you most about the history of the *PV*?

A. This: that none of the many defenders and attackers of the Principle seems to have noticed the ungrammaticality of The Dictum. One can sensibly talk about *using* a method, but "using a meaning" would be a solecism that no native speaker would commit.

A specific method is normally expressible by the use of a verbal infinitive—for instance, "The way to discover whether a door is unlocked is *to turn the handle and push.*" But the clause starting with "to" cannot properly follow "the meaning of 'The door is unlocked is . . . '" On the face of it, The Dictum is as syntactically improper as, say, "The edibility of a pudding is *to taste it.*"

B. Your point is well taken but need not unduly embarrass a verificationist. For he might conceivably replace The Dictum by any of the following formulations:

The meaning of a proposition is *identified* by its verification.

or:

The meaning of a proposition (if any) is whatever does or would verify it.

or even:

To understand a proposition is to know how to verify it.

A. I don't think such changes are trivial. But since we have much to talk about, let me pass on to a couple of questions that continue to bother me.

On reading the earliest pronouncements of the logical positivists, I detected an almost political fervor that reminded me of such slogans as "No taxation without representation" or even "A bas les aristos!" Why were neo-empiricists so zealous in their propagation of the *PV*?

*Meaning and Verification*

B. Your analogy appeals to me. Carnap and Schlick and Neurath (perhaps especially the last) did indeed think of themselves as starting yet another revolution in philosophy.

A. Upsetting an old and decadent order, as it were?

B. Yes. So, The Dictum was at first used iconoclastically, in a negative form that might have been sloganized as:

No meaning without verifiability.

Early verificationists rather enjoyed the scandal caused by accusing metaphysicians, theologians, and old-style moralists of uttering "nonsense" (*Unsinn*).[3]

A. One is reminded, of course, of Hume consigning to the flames any discussion not consisting of "abstract reasoning concerning quantity or number" or "experimental reasoning concerning matters of fact and existence." I suppose the *PV*, in its purgative aspect, was regarded as a radical transformation of classical empiricism?

B. But with a crucial difference. When such earlier empiricists as Hume and Locke asserted that all knowledge was derived from "sensation" or "experience," they did not brand as gibberish the epistemological claims they were rejecting: Hume's enemies (purveyors of "divinity or school metaphysics") could hardly have been guilty of "sophistry and illusion" if they were purveying nonsense.

A. I suppose also that consistent old-style empiricists would have regarded the defining principle of empiricism as itself deriving from experience?

B. Surely. And that would make their principle vulnerable to further empirical investigation, like our present-day discoveries about the behavior of human infants. However, modern neo-empiricists thought of *their PV* as being analytic, and hence certifiable by merely considering the relevant meanings of the terms "meaning" and "verification"—proof, therefore, against empirical refutation.

---

3. In England, A. J. Ayer's *Language, Truth, and Logic* (London, 1936) provoked virulent reactions.

A. That prompts me to raise a question that must have bothered even the friends of verificationism.

How *did* verificationists conceive of the logical status of The Dictum itself—or, in a contemporary idiom, what kind of speech-act can we take them to have been performing when they affirmed that Dictum? You said a moment ago that The Dictum was supposed to be an analytic statement, grounded in definitions of its key terms. Did the verificationists think of those relevant definitions as reflecting actual usage, or as recommended modifications? Were they trying to report the implications of detectable but overlooked semantical data (as one might put it) or were they *proposing* new usages? Or possibly something else?

B. I think the answer has to be that The Dictum was intended to be partly what you have just called a "report" of actual usage, and partly an improvement on it—somewhat in the spirit of what Carnap, much later, called "explication," the replacement of inexact notions by more precise ones, modeled upon what they were to replace, but not identical with them.

A. I take it that a simple proposal to *change* the meanings of the central terms "meaning and verification" would have drawn the sting of the Principle.

B. Quite so. If a self-styled verificationist were to say, ingenuously: "I *propose* that any assertion that does not imply a '*method of verification,*' in a proposed sense of that expression, shall count as nonsensical," no philosopher would be interested.

If somebody claims that animals have inalienable rights, because they are persons, *in a new sense* which he attaches to "person," he contributes nothing to substantive issues about animal rights. (His disreputable, but all too common, maneuver might be called—with apologies to Stevenson—"unpersuasive redefinition.")

A. So you think that Schlick, for instance, thought of himself as simply reporting a sanitized version of actual usage?

B. Well, consider the following, characteristically vigorous pronouncement:

Our view [expressed by The Dictum] proposes to be nothing but a simple statement of the way in which meaning is *actually* assigned

*Meaning and Verification*

to propositions, both in everyday life and in science. There has never been any other way, and it would be a grave error to suppose that we believe we have discovered a new conception of meaning which is contrary to common opinion and which we want to introduce into philosophy. On the contrary, our conception is not only entirely in agreement with, but even derived from, common sense and scientific procedure. Although our criterion of meaning has always been employed in practice, it has rarely been formulated in the past, and this is perhaps the only excuse for the attempts of so many philosophers to deny its feasibility. (*GA*, 341)

A. In a somewhat earlier paper than the one you have just quoted (1932), Schlick described his basic insight ("Einsicht") as being completely "trivial" (*völlig trivial*) (*GA*, 91). Isn't it remarkable in retrospect that a truism could manage to entail extraordinarily paradoxical consequences (as, for instance, in the Circle's notorious discussions of the "mechanical sweetheart")?

B. It may be unfair to saddle Schlick with the Circle's flirtations with radical behaviorism. Remember that the "Einsicht" which you just mentioned was that the sense of every assertion is determined only by the "given" (*"Der Sinn jeder Aussage nur durch das Gegebene bestimmt werden kann"*). Schlick was claiming that the sense of a significant dictum is, ultimately, (*"in letzter linie"*), necessarily determined by immediate experience.

A. I take it that you think that the alleged insight, far from being a truism, is false. But how would you show that?

B. I would want first to make a distinction, unformulated in The Dictum, between the meaning attached by some person to his own or another's assertion (call it a *user's meaning*) and the *standard meaning* of the sentence in question. (Of course, I don't think of somebody's personal meaning as essentially "private": he would normally be able to express what *he* means only by using some sentence having a standard meaning.)

A. I see where you are heading: you are going to invoke a parallel distinction between a person's available verification and the "standard" verification, if any.

B. Quite so. Suppose you were to say, "I have got a headache" and I were to reply, "No, you only think you have!"

A. Quite characteristically!

B. Would The Dictum imply that I was denying the very same proposition that you had asserted? Our respectively available modes of verification differ: you rely upon your feelings, while I observe your ironical smile.

A. So your point is that The Dictum, thus interpreted, requires us, implausibly, to assign different meanings to a first-person assertion and to the corresponding third-person assertion.

B. Which would mean that I wasn't denying your headache avowal. However, similar trouble will arise in connection with assertions whose meanings are not context-dependent. If I were foolish enough to say that selenium was a metal (confusing it with silver), a chemist who had worked with the stuff would correct me at once. But if I persisted, our respective modes of verification would differ: he could rely on memory of chemical experiences, while I would have to consult a dictionary.

A. Then why not take The Dictum, in this case, as alluding to some standard test or criterion for selenium?

B. That would not explain how I, who don't know what the test is, can talk about *selenium*. (And I mean that very substance, not "whatever it is that competent chemists talk about when they say 'selenium.'")

A. I hope you haven't forgotten your promise to offer a counterexample to The Dictum.

B. Well, how about the assertion "After my death, I shall remain conscious?" How could that be *falsified?* And if it could not in principle be falsified, how could it count as being verifiable?[4]

A. I know from my recent reading that bizarre counterexamples like this were evoked against Schlick and other verificationists. But I am surprised that *you*, who are no friend of outré examples, should stoop to this kind of thing. After all, Schlick thought of himself most of the time as explicating the meaning of *scientific* assertions. How about providing a counterexample from sober science?

B. But how are we to authenticate the admissability of such an example? What are the semantical or conceptual constraints on

---

4. Schlick thought it could be verified by following the prescription "Wait until you die!" (*GA*, p. 355). Cf. his remark "'Waiting' is a perfectly legitimate method of verification" (*GA*, p. 345).

*Meaning and Verification*

what you call "sober science?" Are physicists who study cosmogony bombinating in the void? Can it make good verificationist sense to speculate about a big bang billions of years ago, when "time began"? Or, more prosaically, should we count an assertion about the possible extinction of all life in the universe as "nonsensical" in some drastically pejorative sense?

A. I notice that you are reverting to your favorite practice of arguing—if one can call it that—by offering rhetorical questions.

B. Touché!

A. Wouldn't it be fairer to Schlick to concede that he had in mind the "logical analysis" of a limited class of propositions—the "factual" ones of sober science, and not what might be considered fragments of science fantasy?

B. But how does one antecedently identify the class of "factual" propositions without begging the question of verifiability and rendering PV a useless tautology?

A. Have you got some *positive* suggestions, for a change?

B. One might perhaps use as a rough test of *factual* assertion the possibility of attaching a reference to probability. The problematically factual proposition, "God created the world" would then count as meaningful only if "*Probably* God created the world" made sense. But the expanded statement is as problematic as the original. (Is the Argument From Design supported by *factual* premises?)

A. Well, let us not get diverted by your counterexamples. In all this preliminary talk you haven't yet discussed the meaning of "verification" and "verifiability." Are you deliberately dodging what looks like the central issue?

B. Not at all! Let us consider "verification" now. First, then, "verification," as used by the verificationists, seems to have been a rather misleading term of art, differing in intended application from ordinary uses of that rarely used word.

A. How so?

B. My dictionary says that the head-sense of "verify" is "to prove the truth of, as by evidence or testimony." But the intended technical meaning of verifiability includes a possibility of disproof. In its intended philosophical sense, then, falsification is a special case of verification. I would therefore prefer to call possibility of verification-and-falsification *attestability*.

## Verificationism Revisited: A Conversation

A. That seems to me a rather minor point of diction.

B. Well, here is a more substantial observation.

"Verification" must be the *doing* of something: it therefore implies some process of establishing the *truth* (or, in the light of what I said a moment ago, possibly the *falsity*) of the proposition under test. Yet verification (or "attestation") does not have the discovery of truth-value as its proximate objective. Positive attestation of, say, "It is raining now" can indeed show that the assertion in question is true, but if so, the assertion is true *because* it is raining at the time in question. What directly attests that it is now raining is simply that it is now raining: the attested proposition cannot refer to *itself* and *its own* truth-value: it is simply about whether *rain is falling*.

A. Perhaps so. Yet I don't think you have said anything that should seriously worry an unregenerate verificationist.

B. I hope you aren't referring to yourself?

A. Not yet. Still, your sharpshooting almost inclines me to join the verificationist camp. I have a feeling that you are trying to nibble the Verifiability Principle into oblivion. Couldn't you give me a *Grundgedanke*—some Big Thing that you take to be basically wrong with verificationism, however amended?

B. As you know, I am unsympathetic to *Grundgedanken*. However, if I had to single out just one Big Thing that seems, in retrospect, to have been wrong about verificationism, it might be the failure to recognize and cope with a "process-product" equivocation.

A. Details, please!

B. Verification, like anything else *to be done*, is a purposive activity directed to some predetermined goal. (Attesting an assertion is like shooting at a target—or following a recipe for producing a pudding.) In such cases, there is an end in view, to be attained by some appropriate procedure, resulting, if all goes well, in a satisfactory outcome. ("The proof of the pudding is in the eating.")

So we ought to distinguish, scrupulously, between verification as *seeking* and verification as *finding* (or failing to find).

A. You claim, then, that the neo-empiricists didn't notice, or take account of, a rather obvious distinction between, shall we say, a verification-*path* and the terminal verification-*situation*.

37

*Meaning and Verification*

B. Yes, I do. Indeed, one can find them switching in mid-discussion from what I shall distinguish as an *operational* reading of The Dictum to a *situational* one.

A. Which did they adopt?

B. Well, at first the "situational" version, partly because something like that can be found in their principal source, the *Tractatus*—even though it would be misleading to call the author of that book a "verificationist." I think we shall be able to see how that choice encouraged the interpretation of The Dictum as a "truism."

A. Reference, please?

B. A good place to look is in the section of Carnap's monograph *Scheinprobleme in der Philosophie*[5] entitled "Das Kriterium des Sinnes," in which he says:

> Der Sinn einer Aussage besteht darin, das sie einen (denkbaren, nicht notwendig auch bestehenden) Sachverhalt zum Ausdruck bringt. (p. 27)

> [The sense of an assertion consists in its expressing a (conceivable, though not necessarily realized) state of affairs.]

He proceeds to say in effect that the realization of the relevant state of affairs is a necessary and sufficient condition for the assertion to be true.

This "criterion of sense" obviously derives from such *Tractatus* remarks as:

> Der Satz zeigt wie es sich verhält, wenn er wahr ist. Und er sagt, daß es sich so verhält. (4.022)
> Einen Satz verstehen, heißt, wissen was der Fall ist wenn er wahr ist. (4.024)

A. Well, isn't that a rather attractive idea?

B. It certainly appealed strongly to the author of the *Tractatus*. It is indeed tempting to think that a particular assertion, say "Reagan's term will end in 1984," points to, or aims at, some

---

5. Carnap, *Scheinprobleme in der Philosophie* (Berlin, 1928).

conceivable state-of-affairs or "situation" that will, one hopes, be realized in 1984. So we might be led to say that:

> "Reagan's term will end in 1984" means that Reagan's term will end in 1984.

A. Self-evident, my dear Watson! It may not be very illuminating, but surely it is right (on a certain construction of 'means')?

B. No. What's wrong with it from a philosophical point of view is the overarching vision, detectable in the *Tractatus*, of the "facts" (*Sachverhalte*) as being constitutive parts of "reality" (*die Wirklichkeit*), objectively awaiting inspection. Consider such remarks as:

> Die Wirklichkeit wird mit dem Satz verglichen. (4.05) Nur dadurch kann der Satz wahr oder falsch sein, indem er ein Bild der Wirklichkeit ist. (4.06)
> Was das Bild darstellt ist seinen Sinn. (2.221) Um zu erkennen, ob das Bild wahr oder falsch ist, müssen wir es mit der Wirklichkeit vergleichen. (2.223)

A. I take it you don't like the metaphor of "comparison?"

B. Quite. We don't normally look *at* a proposition or a sentence and compare it point for point with "reality"—as one might, with floor plan in hand, check the accuracy of its representation of the actual floor. The normal case is that of having the relevant assertion in mind and then—if the attestation succeeds—coming to know that things are as specified.

A. But wasn't that what Wittgenstein was saying—metaphorically, if you like?

B. Not altogether. There is also a background mythology of *facts*: they constitute "the world," whether or not they are asserted to be facts.

Once we discard the mythology, and try to express the general form of my Reagan example, without its factitious mythology, we get only the formula:

> '$p$' means that $p$.

*Meaning and Verification*

But this is a useless truism,[6] serving no identifiable purpose, whether inside or outside philosophical discussion. Worst of all for friends of verificationism, it cannot discriminate sense from nonsense. A purveyor of nonsense can cheerfully agree that:

> "The Absolute is pink" means that the Absolute is pink.

A. How fast you go when ontology rears its ugly head! (I wish we had the time to consider your abusive description of Wittgenstein's *Tractatus* ontology as a "mythology.")

B. Isn't that how he himself thought of it in his later investigations?

A. Well, let that go, for now. I presume that you think that what you have called the "operational reading" of The Dictum escapes from your latest strictures?

B. Not at all. Parallel difficulties arise from taking The Dictum to mean something like:

> '$p$' means whatever has to be done to establish p.

Awkward consequences arise in applying this operational version of The Dictum to a particular instance. Waiving for the moment the impossibility of specifying the particular "verification path" without also specifying the culminating stage of "comparing" the $p$ in question with reality, the trouble is that in looking for the attestation situation we must *already understand '$p$.'*

A. Couldn't your objection be met by only *mentioning* the sentence expressing the proposition in question? For instance:

> "The pubs are opening now" means whatever we would need to do in order to establish that that sentence is correct.

B. That is merely a pretentious way of saying:

> "The pubs are opening now" means: If we were to investigate, we should find that the pubs are opening now.

---

6. The reader might care to consult my further examination of the "truism" in "Verificationism and Wittgenstein's Reflections on Mathematics," *Revue Internationale de Philosophie* 88–89 (1969), especially at pp. 286–87.

A. Which they are! I think you are beginning to repeat yourself: perhaps we would do better to abandon argument for liquid refreshment. But before I treat you to a beer, won't you say something in favor of The Dictum—and of verificationism? Isn't there some way of understanding it that will not imply that the young Wittgenstein (not to mention Peirce and other pragmatists and operationalists) had nothing valuable to contribute?

B. Well. Wittgenstein, as reported by Moore, took a more promising line when he said, "The sense of a proposition is the way in which it is verified," but later added that he meant:

> "You can determine the meaning of a proposition by asking how it is verified" and went on to say, "This is necessarily a mere rule of thumb, because 'verification' means different things, and because in some cases the question 'How is it verified?' makes no sense."[7]

The Dictum, thus interpreted, as a "rule of thumb" for helping to understand the meaning of problematic assertions, does have a limited use. However, I would want to view the maxim as formulating a special case of a more general maxim, say:

> To understand the meaning of a problematic term (like "the meaning of a sentence") consider the various linguistic contexts in which that term can sensibly occur.

To use that old analogy of chess: we don't understand what "the King" means unless we also understand what "moving the King," "checking the King," "taking the King out of check," "checkmating the King," and so on mean. And the same goes for the problematic expression "the meaning of a sentence." In my old example, we need to understand what it means to "*believe* that it is raining now" and "there is *reason to doubt* whether it is raining now," and so on and so forth. Frege's principle that a word has meaning only in the context of a sentence needs to be generalized to something like:

> Any expression (not only names and descriptions, but also sentences) is intelligible only in the context of a language.

7. G. E. Moore, *Philosophical Papers* (New York, 1959), p. 266.

*Meaning and Verification*

I take it that Wittgenstein had something of the sort in mind when he said:

> Asking whether and how a proposition can be verified is only a particular way of asking "How do you mean that?" The answer is a contribution to the *grammar* of the proposition. (*Philosophical Investigations*, sect. 353; emphasis added)

Of course, Wittgenstein doesn't mean "surface grammar" or even, I think, the "deep structure" of contemporary grammarians. Further exploration of the largely unformulated rules controlling the significant uses of philosophically interesting words remains, in spite of Wittgenstein's splendid legacy, an important and unfinished philosophical task.

A. You sound as if you are drawing to a close. Are you then going to say nothing about the *observational* emphasis in the verificationists' appeal to "verification?"

B. Well, sufficient unto the day is the discussion thereof. I suppose you might say that I have been making somewhat scattered remarks about a *general* theory of meaning as verifiability; the *special* supplementary theory, exploring connections between verifiability and factual meaning, would need more time than we have got.

A. Not long ago, Ayer, in reviewing the main doctrines of his *Language, Truth, and Logic*, said:

> [T]he verification principle, on which so much depended, was far too loosely formulated. . . . Even so, . . . I still broadly adhere to what may be called the verificatory approach. So indeed does a great deal of subsequent philosophy. . . . The verification principle is seldom mentioned and when it is mentioned it is usually scorned; it continues however, to be put to work.[8]

Do you agree?

B. Well, you know by now that I agree with Ayer's first remark. But I would insist that no plausible and precise revision of The Dictum is available. I am puzzled in retrospect to understand how

---

8. A. J. Ayer, *Part of My Life* (New York, 1977), pp. 155–56.

anything as elusive as the original principle could continue to "be put to work." (I wish Ayer had provided an example.)

A. You asked me some time ago what had particularly struck me about the extraordinary career of the Verifiability Principle. Let me return that same question to you.

B. I find at least two things remarkable about what might be called the rise and decline of verificationism. One is that philosophers as talented and gifted as the members of the Vienna Circle, who properly insisted upon the need for clarity and precision in philosophical investigation, should have been content to adhere so long to a formula as shoddy as The Dictum, and to respond to searching criticism by "ad-hoc-ery"—opportunistic adjustments to immediate challenges, without reconsideration of the underlying assumptions.

Second, that avowed empiricists should have behaved so much like old-style rationalists, in giving only perfunctory attention to how scientists and nonspecialists actually *use* words and express concepts. For all the insistence of the logical positivists upon the need to analyze language, you will find no account taken of the spectacular advances that were being made in linguistics. And verificationists' views of how science is actually conducted (especially in such flourishing areas as biology) seem in retrospect extraordinarily schematic and oversimplified.

A. Are things better now?

B. I am sure they are. The heirs of Logical Positivism do nowadays at least try to use the resources of contemporary linguistics and work with somewhat more realistic conceptions than their predecessors had of how scientists actually work.

A. And the moral you draw from this history . . . ?

B. That empiricists should take their empiricism seriously, without allowing their initial insights to petrify into dogmas.

# METAPHOR

# 3
## More about Metaphor

This paper is intended to supplement the earlier study in which I introduced and defended an "interaction view of metaphor."[1] A reader unfamiliar with that study will find a summary in the section entitled "The Interaction View Revisited."

I shall try here to amplify my original formulation by explicating the grounds of the metaphors of "interaction," "filtering," and "screening," which I used in trying to understand how metaphorical statements work. I shall add some suggestions about the relations of a metaphor to its grounding resemblances and analogies (somewhat neglected in *Metaphor*), with the hope of also shedding some further light on the connections between metaphors and models.

This occasion gives me an opportunity to take some notice of the numerous criticisms, mostly friendly, which *Metaphor* has received since its original publication. Pleased though I am at the widespread acceptance of the *interaction view*, I agree with Monroe Beardsley, Ted Cohen, Paul Ricœur, and others that more work will be needed before the power and limitations of this approach to the subject can be fully appreciated.

---

This essay is a slightly modified version of one that appeared under the same title in *Dialectica* 31 (1977), pp. 431–57.

1. Max Black, "Metaphor," in *Models and Metaphors* (Ithaca, N.Y., 1962), ch. 3; hereafter cited as *Metaphor*.

## Reasons for Current Interest in Metaphor

John Middleton Murry's essay "Metaphor"[2] opens with the remark "Discussions of metaphor—there are not many of them—often strike us at first as superficial." Today both comments would be inappropriate. The extraordinary volume of papers and books on the subject produced during the past forty years might suggest that the subject is inexhaustible.[3]

Warren Shibles's useful bibliography[4] has entries running to nearly three hundred pages and contains perhaps as many as four thousand titles. As for these discussions being superficial, one might rather complain today of ungrounded profundity, because so many writers, agreeing with Murry that "metaphor is as ultimate as speech itself, and speech as ultimate as thought" (p. 1), rapidly draw ontological morals, while leaving the nature of metaphorical speech and thought tantalizingly obscure.

In the inconclusive debate between the appreciators and depreciators of metaphor, the former nowadays score most points. But they are characteristically prone to inflation. As W. Nowottny puts it:

> Current criticism often takes metaphor *au grand sérieux*, as a peephole on the nature of transcendental reality, a prime means by which the imagination can see into the life of things.

She adds:

> [T]his attitude makes it difficult to see the workings of those metaphors which deliberately emphasize the frame, offering themselves as deliberate fabrications, as a prime means of seeing into the life

---

2. John Middleton Murry, "Metaphor," in *Countries of the Mind* (Oxford, 1931), pp. 1–16.

3. This suggestion is sometimes attributed to Michel Bréal. See his *Essai de semantique* (Paris, 1899), p. 125. But the subject he called *infini* was the special one of the influence of metaphors upon the extension and renewal of a standard lexicon, of which he provides numerous illustrations.

4. Warren Shibles, *Metaphor: An Annotated Bibliography and History* (Whitewater, Wis., 1971).

*More about Metaphor*

not of things but of the creative human consciousness, framer of its own world.⁵

Enthusiastic friends of metaphor are indeed prone to various kinds of inflation, ready to see metaphor everywhere, in the spirit of Carlyle, who said:

> Examine language; what, if you expect some primitive elements of natural sound, what is it all but metaphors, recognized as such or no longer recognized; still fluid and florid or now solid-grown and colourless? If these same primitive garments are the osseous fixtures in the Flesh-Garment Language then are metaphors its muscle and living integuments.⁶

This quotation illustrates a pervasive tendency for writers, including myself in *Metaphor*, to frame their basic insights in metaphorical terms.

A related inflationary thrust is shown in a persistent tendency, found in Aristotle's still influential treatment, and manifest in as recent a discussion as Nelson Goodman's *Languages of Art*,⁷ to regard all figurative uses of language as metaphorical, and in this way to ignore the important distinctions between metaphor and such other figures of speech as simile, metonymy, and synecdoche.

To make a sufficiently intricate topic still harder to handle, the depreciators tend to focus upon relatively trivial examples ("Man is a wolf") that conform to the traditional "substitution view," and the special form of it that I called the "comparison view,"⁸ whereas appreciators, in their zeal to establish "that metaphor is the omnipresent principle of language,"⁹ tend to dwell upon excitingly suggestive but obscure examples from Shakespeare, Donne, Hopkins, or Dylan Thomas, to the neglect of simpler

---

5. W. Nowottny, *The Language Poets Use* (London, 1962), p. 89.
6. S. J. Brown, *The World of Imagery* (London, 1927), p. 41.
7. Nelson Goodman, *Languages of Art* (Indianapolis, 1968).
8. See my *Models and Metaphors*, esp. pp. 30–37.
9. I. A. Richards, "Metaphor," in *The Philosophy of Rhetoric* (Oxford, 1936), p. 92. Richards says that this "can be shown by mere observation."

instances that also require attention in a comprehensive theory.

Although I am on the side of the appreciators, who dwell upon what Empson and Ricœur call "vital" metaphors, I think their opponents (typically philosophers, scientists, mathematicians, and logicians) are right in asking for less "vital" or less "creative" metaphors to be considered. It may well be a mistaken strategy to treat profound metaphors as paradigms.

In what follows, I shall steer a middle course, taking as points of departure metaphors complex enough to invite analysis, yet sufficiently transparent for such analysis to be reasonably uncontroversial. My interest in this paper is particularly directed toward the "cognitive aspects" of certain metaphors, whether in science, philosophy, theology, or ordinary life, and their power to present in a distinctive and irreplaceable way, insight into "how things are" (for which, see the section entitled "Can a Metaphorical Statement Ever Reveal 'How Things Are'?"). I shall leave the "poetic metaphors" invoked by Nowottny for another occasion.

What Is the "Mystery" of Metaphor?

One writer, who might be speaking for many, says, "Among the mysteries of human speech, metaphor has remained one of the most baffling."[10] But what is this supposed mystery? Given the prevalence or, if we are to trust Richards and many other thinkers, the ubiquity of metaphor, metaphorical discourse might well seem no more mysterious than singing or dancing—and, one might add, no more improper or deviant.

In the sentence following the one I have quoted, Father Boyle refers to the "odd predilection for asserting a thing to be what it is not." So perhaps the "mystery" is simply that, *taken as literal*, a metaphorical statement appears to be perversely asserting something to be what it is plainly known not to be. (And that makes

---

10. R. R. Boyle, "The Nature of Metaphor," *Modern Schoolman* 31 (1954), p. 257.

the metaphor user look like a liar or a deceiver.) When Juliet says to Romeo, "The light that shines comes from thine eyes," she surely cannot *really mean* that his eyeballs are lighting up the chamber; when Wallace Stevens says, "A poem is a pheasant," he cannot *really* mean that it flaps its wings and has a long tail—for such things are plainly false and absurd. But such "absurdity" and "falsity" are of the essence: in their absence, we should have no metaphor but merely a literal utterance. So a metaphor user, unless he is merely babbling, would seem, according to the ancient formula, to "say one thing and mean another." But why?

An intelligent child, hearing his scientist father refer to a "field of force," might ask—but with a twinkle in his eye, one hopes—"And who plows it?" In order to feel the supposed "mystery," one needs to recapture the naiveté of somebody who takes metaphorical utterances to be literal or the false naiveté of someone who pretends to do so. But to assume that a metaphorical utterance presents something as what it is plainly not—or to assume that its producer really does intend to say one thing while meaning something else—is to beg disastrously a prime question by accepting the misleading view of a metaphor as some kind of deviation or aberration from proper usage.

Somebody seriously making a metaphorical statement—say, "The Lord is my Shepherd"—might reasonably claim that he meant just what he said, having chosen the words most apt to express his thought, attitudes, and feelings, and was by no means guilty of uttering a crass absurdity. Such a position cannot be rejected out of hand.

The danger of an approach that treats literal utterance as an unproblematic standard, while regarding metaphorical utterance as problematic or mysterious by contrast, is that it tends to encourage reductionist theories: As the plain man might say, "If the metaphor producer didn't mean what he said, why didn't he say something else?" We are headed for the blind alley taken by those innumerable followers of Aristotle who have supposed metaphors to be replaceable by literal translations.

A sympathetic way of following Father Boyle's lead might be to start by asking what distinguishes a metaphorical statement from a literal one. That, of course, assumes that there is at least a prima facie and observable difference between metaphorical and literal statements—a donnée that seems to me initially less problematic than it does to some theorists. When a writer says, "Men are verbs, not nouns," a reader untrammeled by theoretical preconceptions about the ubiquity of metaphor will immediately recognize that "verbs" and "nouns" are not being used literally. Dictionaries do not include men as a special case of verbs, and a competent speaker will not list them as paradigm cases of the application of that word. And so in general, it would be relatively easy to devise tests, for those who want them, of the literal meaning of the word that is the metaphorical "focus" of a metaphorical utterance. Tacit knowledge of such literal meaning induces the characteristic feeling of dissonance or "tension" between the focus and its literal "frame."

Starting so, and acknowledging a clear prima facie difference between literal and metaphorical uses of expressions, need not, however, prejudge the validity of some "deeper" insight that might eventually reject the commonsensical distinction between the literal and the metaphorical as superficial and ultimately indefensible. But such a revisionist view needs the support of a thorough exploration of the implicit rationale of the commonsense distinction. An effort to do so will naturally concern itself with crucial supplementary questions about the point of using metaphors and, more generally, about the distinctive powers of metaphorical discourse.

Some writers, notably Coleridge, but not he alone, have imputed a peculiarly "creative" role to metaphor (for which, see the section entitled "Are Metaphors Ever 'Creative'?"). That a puzzle or mystery might be perceived in this connection can be supported by the following train of thought. A successful metaphor is *realized* in discourse, is embodied in the given "text," and need not be treated as a riddle. So the writer or speaker is employing conventional means to produce a nonstandard effect, while using only the standard syntactic and semantic resources of his speech community. Yet the meaning of an interesting metaphor is typically new or "creative," not inferable from the standard lexicon. A major task for theorists of metaphor, then, is to explain how such an outcome—striking for all its familiarity—is brought about.

We may usefully consider, for the sake of contrast, the situation of a participant in a rule-governed practice more tightly constrained than speech—say the game of chess. There, too, a creative aspect is readily discernible, because even if all the mistakes are waiting to be discovered (as a master once said) a player must still search for and ultimately *choose* his move: In most chess positions, there is no decision procedure and no demonstrably "correct" move. Yet the player's scope for creativity is sharply limited by the game's inflexible rules, which provide him always with a finite and well-defined set of options.

Imagine now a variation, say "epi-chess," in which a player would have the right to move any piece as if it were another of equal or inferior value (a bishop moving for once like a knight, say, or a pawn)—*provided the opponent accepted such a move.* There we have a primitive model of conversation and discourse, where almost any "move" is acceptable if one can get away with it; that is, if a competent receiver will accept it. But even here there are *some* constraints upon creativity: one cannot couple any two nouns at random and be sure to produce an effective metaphor. (If the reader doubts this, let him try to make sense of "a chair is a syllogism." In the absence of some specially constructed context, this must surely count as a failed metaphor.)

But what is a "creative," rule-violating metaphor producer really trying to do? And what is a competent hearer expected to do in response to such a move?

In *Metaphor*, I suggested that such questions, and most of the others posed by theorists of metaphor, might be regarded as concerned with "the 'logical grammar' of 'metaphor' and words having related meaning"; or as expressing "attempts to become clearer about some uses of the word 'metaphor'" (p. 25); or as the start of an effort "to analyze the notion of metaphor" (p. 26). Although this semantic emphasis has alienated some of my critics, I see no particular harm in it. There would be no substantial difference in an approach that was conceived, in a more ontological idiom, as an effort to "become clearer about the nature of metaphor." Indeed, I would regard the two formulas as equivalent.

*Metaphor*

## Identifying the Targets

The reader will have noticed my references to metaphorical statements. Indeed, my standing concern is with full metaphorical statements and, derivatively, with "statement-ingredients" (words or phrases used metaphorically) only as they occur in *specific* and relatively complete acts of expression and communication. (Hereafter, "metaphor" is usually short for "metaphorical statement.") A "statement," in my intended sense, will be identified by quoting a whole sentence, or a set of sentences, together with as much of the relevant verbal context, or the nonverbal setting, as may be needed for an adequate grasp of the actual or imputed speaker's meaning. I use "meaning" here for whatever a competent hearer may be said to have grasped when he succeeds in responding adequately to the actual or hypothetical verbal action consisting in the serious utterance of the sentence(s) in question.

As examples of such identifications of metaphorical statements, I offer:

(1) "L'homme n'est qu'un roseau, le plus faible de la nature, mais c'est un roseau pensant" (Pascal in the *Pensées*)—or, more briefly, Pascal's metaphor of man as a thinking reed.
(2) "You are a metaphor and they are lies/Or there true least where their knot chance unfurls" (William Empson, *Letter V*).
(3) Ezra Pound's metaphor of education as sheepherding (in his *ABC of Reading*, passim).

Of these metaphors, the last is relatively the most independent of its context and might be sufficiently identified, with suppression of Pound's name, as "the metaphor of education as sheepherding." Yet justice to Pound's view might demand citation of relevant passages in his tract. Textual elaboration is more obviously needed to appreciate Pascal's deceptively simple metaphor or Empson's characteristically obscure one.

I propose to distinguish what is identified merely by a formula like "the metaphor of *A* as *B*," without further specification of its contextual use, as a metaphor-*theme*, regarded as an abstraction from the metaphorical statements in which it does or might occur. A metaphor-theme is available for repeated use, adaptation, and modification by a variety of speakers or thinkers on any number of specific occasions.[11]

One danger in attending mainly to what I have called metaphor-themes is that of postulating a standard response to a given metaphorical statement—a response determined by linguistic, conceptual, cultural, or other conventions. Such a view is untenable because a metaphorical statement involves a rule violation: There can be no rules for "creatively" violating rules.[12] And that is why there can be no *dictionary* (though there might be a thesaurus) of metaphors.

Any attempt to be more precise about the identifying and individuating criteria for metaphorical statements will be embarrassed by the following difficulty. The *very same* metaphorical statement, as I wish to use that expression, may appropriately receive a number of different and even partially conflicting readings. Thus Empson's metaphor, reproduced above, might be taken by one reader, but not another, as imputing falsity to the person addressed. We might choose to say that both were right about two different metaphors expressed in Empson's words; or, less plausibly, that one reader must have been mistaken. There is an ines-

---

11. It might be thought puzzling that while the act of producing a metaphorical statement is a datable event, its semantic content can be described, referred to, and discussed at any time: consequently, what by definition seems to be subjective, as produced by a particular speaker or thinker, has an *import*, as one might say, that is sufficiently stable or objective—in spite of violating the background linguistic conventions—to be available for subsequent analysis, interpretation, and criticism. But is this really more puzzling than the fact that what a tennis player did in his last serve can be talked about (more or less) at any subsequent time?

12. For this reason, my analogy of "epi-chess" may be somewhat misleading. For in that game, there was a "super-rule" of sorts that determined *how* and *when* the rules of ordinary chess might be violated. In view of what looks like the essential lawlessness of metaphorical transgression, I am less sanguine than other writers about the prospects of treating the production of a metaphorical statement as a speech act in Austin's sense. I, too, wish to attend particularly to what a metaphor user is doing and what he expects his auditor to do. But I see little profit in modeling this primal situation on that of a promise giver (Austin's paradigm case), where the consequences of the performative statement are determined by a speech community's *conventions*.

capable indeterminacy in the notion of a *given* metaphorical-statement, so long as we count its import as part of its essence.

I hope these brief terminological remarks will serve for the present occasion. In what follows, I shall not insist pedantically upon using the qualifiers "-statement" or "-theme," usually leaving the context to resolve any possible ambiguity.


## On Classifying Metaphors; and the Importance of Emphasis and Resonance

Given the prevalence of metaphorical statements and their manifest versatility, a student of the subject would find some generally accepted classification helpful in making even the simplest distinctions. But at present, he is in an even worse situation than a biologist before Linnaeus. For the only entrenched classification is grounded in the trite opposition (itself expressed metaphorically) between "dead" and "live" metaphors. This is no more helpful than, say, treating a corpse as a special case of a person: A so-called dead metaphor is not a metaphor at all, but merely an expression that no longer has a pregnant metaphorical use.

A competent reader is not expected to recognize such a familiar expression as "falling in love" as a metaphor, to be taken *au grand séieux*. Indeed, it is doubtful whether that expression was ever more than a case of catachresis (using an idiom to fill a gap in the lexicon).

If the "actuality" of a metaphor, its possessing the distinctive characteristics, whatever they may be, of genuine metaphorical efficacy, is important enough to be marked, one might consider replacing the dead and alive contrast by a set of finer discriminations: distinguishing perhaps between expressions whose etymologies, genuine or fancied, suggest a metaphor beyond resuscitation (a muscle as a little mouse, *musculus*); those where the original, now usually unnoticed, metaphor can be usefully restored (obligation as involving some kind of bondage); and those, the objects of my present interest, that are, and are perceived to be, actively metaphoric. Appropriate labels might be:

"extinct," "dormant," and "active" metaphors. But not much is to be expected of this schema or any more finely tuned substitute. (I shall be concerned hereafter only with metaphors needing no artificial respiration, recognized by speaker and hearer as authentically "vital" or active.)

Given an active metaphorical statement, it would be useful to discriminate two aspects, which I shall call *emphasis* and *resonance*. A metaphorical utterance is *emphatic*, in my intended sense, to the degree that its producer will allow no variation upon or substitute for the words used—and especially not for what in *Metaphor* I called the "focus," the salient word or expression, whose occurrence in the literal frame invests the utterance with metaphorical force. Plausible opposites to "emphatic" might include: "expendable," "optional," "decorative," and "ornamental." (Relatively dispensable metaphors are often no more than literary or rhetorical flourishes that deserve no more serious attention than musical grace notes.) Emphatic metaphors are intended to be dwelt upon for the sake of their unstated implications: Their producers need the receiver's cooperation in perceiving what lies *behind* the words used.

How far such interpretative response can reach will depend upon the complexity and power of the metaphor-theme in question: Some metaphors, even famous ones, barely lend themselves to implicative elaboration, while others, perhaps less interesting, prove relatively rich in background implications. For want of a better label, I shall call metaphorical utterances that support a high degree of implicative elaboration *resonant*.

Resonance and emphasis are matters of degree. They are not independent: Highly emphatic metaphors tend to be highly resonant (though there are exceptions), while the unemphatic occurrence of a markedly resonant metaphor is apt to produce a dissonance, sustained by irony or some similarly distancing operation.

Finally, I propose to call a metaphor that is both markedly emphatic and resonant a *strong metaphor*. My purpose in the remainder of this paper is to analyze the raison d'être and the mode of operation of strong metaphors, treating those that are relatively "weak" on account of relatively low emphasis or resonance as etiolated specimens.

*Metaphor*

A weak metaphor might be compared to an unfunny joke, or an unilluminating philosophical epigram: One understands the unsuccessful or failed verbal actions in the light of what *would be* funny, illuminating, or what have you. Yet if all jokes are intended to be funny, and fail to the degree that they are not, not all metaphors aim at strength, and some may be none the worse for that.

Consider the following example from a letter of Virginia Woolf to Lytton Strachey:

> How you weave in every scrap—my god what scraps!—of interest to be had, like (you must pardon the metaphor) a snake insinuating himself through innumerable golden rings—(Do snakes?—I hope so).[13]

The snake metaphor used here should certainly count as weak in my terminology, because Strachey was intended to take the rich implicative background lightly.

### The Interaction View Revisited

The interaction view which I presented in *Metaphor* was there characterized as an attempt "to become clearer about some uses of the word 'metaphor'—or, if one prefers the material model, to analyze the notion of metaphor" (pp. 25–26). In retrospect, I would prefer to think of my position as a help to understanding how strong metaphorical statements *work*. But this shift of formulation from conceptual analysis to a functional analysis, though potentially important, need not detain us.

The merits of the interaction view, a development and modification of I. A. Richards's valuable insights, should be weighed against those of its only available alternatives—the traditional "substitution view" and "comparison view" (a special case of the former). Briefly stated, the substitution view regards "the entire sentence that is the locus of the metaphor as replacing some set of literal sentences" (p. 31); while the comparison view takes the

---

13. N. Nicolson and J. Trautmann, eds., *The Letters of Virginia Woolf*, vol. 2, *1912–1922* (New York, 1976), p. 205.

imputed literal paraphrase to be a statement of some similarity or analogy, and so takes every metaphor to be a condensed or elliptic simile (pp. 35–36).

The reader will notice that both of these views treat metaphors as *unemphatic*, in my terminology—in principle, expendable if one disregards the incidental pleasures of stating figuratively what might just as well have been said literally.

A brief summary of the preferred interaction view might consist of the following claims, based upon the concluding summary of *Metaphor* (pp. 44–45). I reproduce the original formulations, with minor improvements, appending afterthoughts in each case.

1. A metaphorical statement has two distinct subjects, to be identified as the "primary" subject and the "secondary" one.

    In *Metaphor*, I spoke instead of the "principal" and "subsidiary" subjects. The duality of reference is marked by the contrast between the metaphorical statement's *focus* (the word or words used nonliterally) and the surrounding literal *frame*.

2. The secondary subject is to be regarded as a system rather than an individual thing.

    Thus, I think of Wallace Stevens's remark "Society is a sea" as being not so much about the sea (considered as a thing) as about a system of relationships (the "implicative complex" discussed below) signaled by the presence of the word "sea" in the sentence in question. (In *Metaphor*, I proposed that the primary subject, also, be taken as a system. But it seems in retrospect needlessly paradoxical, though not plainly mistaken, to say that Stevens was viewing society, too, as a system of social relationships.) In retrospect, the intended emphasis upon "systems," rather than upon "things" or "ideas" (as in Richards), looks like one of the chief novelties in the earlier study.

3. The metaphorical utterance works by "projecting upon" the primary subject a set of "associated implications," comprised in the implicative complex, that are predictable of the secondary subject.

    The label "implicative complex" is new. "Projection" is, of course, a metaphor that will need further discussion. In the earlier study, I spoke of a "system of associated commonplaces" (which later provoked some pointed criticisms by Paul Ricœur). My notion was that the secondary subject, in a way partly depending upon the context of metaphorical use, determines a set of what Aristotle called *endoxa*, current opinions shared by members of a certain speech community. But I also emphasized, as I should certainly wish to do now, that a metaphor producer may introduce a novel and nonplatitudinous "implication-complex."

4. The maker of a metaphorical statement selects, emphasizes, suppresses, and organizes features of the primary subject by applying to it statements isomorphic with the members of the secondary subject's implicative complex.

The mechanisms of such "projection" (a still serviceable metaphor) are discussed and illustrated in the next section.

5. In the context of a particular metaphorical statement, the two subjects "interact" in the following ways: (a) the presence of the primary subject incites the hearer to select some of the secondary subject's properties; and (b) invites him to construct a parallel implication-complex that can fit the primary subject; and (c) reciprocally induces parallel changes in the secondary subject.

This may be considered a crux for the interaction view (an attempted explication of Richards's striking image of the "interanimation of words"). Although I speak figuratively here of the *subjects* interacting, such an outcome is of course produced in the minds of the speaker and hearer: It is they who are led to engage in selecting, organizing, and projecting. I think of a metaphorical statement (even a weak one) as a verbal action essentially demanding *uptake*, a creative response from a competent reader. In *Metaphor*, I said—scandalizing some of my subsequent critics—that the imputed interaction involves "shifts in meaning of words belonging to the same family or system as the metaphorical expression" (p. 45). I meant, of course, a shift in the *speaker's* meaning—and the corresponding *hearer's* meaning—what both of them understand by words, as used on the particular occasion.

## How Metaphorical Statements Work

Consider "Marriage is a zero-sum game." In this relatively "active" metaphor the implication-complex might be spelled out somewhat as follows:

(G1) A "game" is a *contest*;
(G2) between two opponents;
(G3) in which one player can win only at the expense of the other.

*More about Metaphor*

The corresponding system of imputed claims about marriage depends crucially upon the interpretations given to "contest," "opponents," and especially to "winning." One might try:

(M1) A marriage is a sustained struggle;
(M2) between two contestants;
(M3) in which the rewards (power? money? satisfaction?) of one contestant are gained only at the other's expense.[14]

Here, the "projected" propositions can be taken literally—or almost so, no matter what one thinks of their plausibility (the metaphor's aptness not being here in question).

Such a heavy-handed analysis of course neglects the ambience of the secondary subject, the suggestions and valuations that necessarily attach themselves to a game-theory view of marriage, and thereby suffuse the receiver's perception of it: A marriage that can be seen as a competitive "game" of skill and calculation is not the kind made in heaven.

The relations between the three members of the implication complex (G1–3) in this relatively simple example and their correlated statements about marriage (M1–3) are a mixed lot. M2 might be said to predicate of marriage precisely what G2 does of a two-person game (with some hesitation about the matching of "opponents" and "contestants"); but in the shift from G1 to M1 it seems more plausible to discern some similarity rather than strict identity; and in M3, finally, "gain" must surely have an extended sense, by contrast with its sense in G3, since marital struggles usually do not end in clear-cut conventional victories. The difficulty in making firm and decisive judgments on such points is, I think, present in *all* cases of metaphorical statement. Since we must necessarily read "behind the words," we cannot

---

14. To these might be added the following optional implications, which would readily occur to somebody familiar with game theory, though not to a layman:
(G4) There is no rational procedure for winning in a single play.
(G5) A "maximin" strategy (playing to minimize possible losses) may, though controversially, be considered rational.
(G6) Playing a long-run "mixed strategy" (alternating available moves randomly but in a predetermined frequency) is (again, controversially) a "solution."

These further implications would, of course, strengthen the metaphor and heighten its interest.

set firm bounds to the admissible interpretations: Ambiguity is a necessary byproduct of the metaphor's suggestiveness.

So far as I can see, after scrutinizing many examples, the relations between the meanings of the corresponding key words of the two implication-complexes can be classified as (a) identity, (b) extension, typically ad hoc, (c) similarity, (d) analogy, or (e) what might be called "metaphorical coupling" (where, as often happens, the original metaphor implicates subordinate metaphors).

Let us now idealize the connection between the two implication-complexes ($G$ and $M$) in the following way: $G$ consists of certain statements, say $Pa$, $Qb$, ..., and $aRb$, $cSd$, ..., while $M$ comprises corresponding statements $P'a'$, $Q'b'$, ..., and $a'R'b'$, $c'S'd'$, ..., (where $P$ is uniquely correlated with $P'$, $a$ with $a'$, $R$ with $R'$, and so on). Then the two systems have, as mathematicians say, the same "structure"; they are isomorphic.[15] One important deviation from the mathematical conception is that $G$ is linked with $M$ by a "mixed lot" of projective relations, as we saw in the game-marriage example, and not (as typically in mathematical contexts) by a single projective relation.

With such conceptions to hand, we need not speak metaphorically about "projecting" the secondary system. Viewed in this way (and neglecting the important suggestions and connotations—the ambience, tone, and attitudes that are also projected upon $M$), $G$ is precisely what I have called in the past an "analog-model."[16] I am now impressed, as I was insufficiently so when composing *Metaphor*, by the tight connections between the notions of models and metaphors. Every implication-complex supported by a metaphor's secondary subject, I now think, is a *model* of the ascriptions imputed to the primary subject: Every metaphor is the tip of a submerged model.

---

15. For a lucid exposition of this notion, see Rolf Eberle, "Models, Metaphors, and Formal Interpretations," in *The Myth of Metaphor*, ed. C. M. Turbayne, rev. ed. (Columbia, S.C., 1970), pp. 219–33.

16. Cf. my "Models and Archetypes," in *Models and Metaphors*. This conception might, accordingly, be regarded as a generalization of S. J. Brown's view of metaphor as an "analogy between ... two relations" (*World of Imagery*, p. 71). I differ from him in admitting any number of predicates and relations in isomorphic correlation—and in laying less stress than he does upon analogy, that tantalizingly suggestive but obscure notion.

## Metaphors and Similes

I have said that there is a similarity, analogy, or, more generally, an identity of structure between the secondary implication-complex of a metaphor and the set of assertions—the primary implication-complex—that it maps. In "Poverty is a crime," "crime" and "poverty" are nodes of isomorphic networks, in which assertions about crime are correlated one-to-one with corresponding statements about poverty.

Hence, every metaphor may be said to mediate an analogy or structural correspondence. (That is the correct insight behind the classical comparison view of metaphor as elliptical or truncated simile.) Hence, also, every metaphorical statement may be said to implicate a likeness-statement and a comparison-statement, each weaker than the original metaphorical statement. ("I didn't say that he is *like* an echo; I said and meant that he *is* an echo!") But to perceive that a metaphor is grounded in similarity and analogy is not to agree with Whatley that "the simile or comparison may be considered as differing *in form only* from a metaphor" or with Bain that "the metaphor is a comparison implied in the use of a term."[17] Implication is not the same as covert identity: Looking at a scene through blue spectacles is different from *comparing* that scene with something else.

To call "Poverty is a crime" a simile or comparison is either to say too little or too much. In a given context of utterance, "Poverty is like a crime" may still be figurative, and hardly more than a stylistic variant upon the original metaphorical statement. Burns might have said, "My Love is a red, red rose" instead of "My Love is like a red, red rose," if the meter had permitted, with little semantic difference, if any. But to suppose that the metaphorical statement is an abstract or précis of a literal point-by-point comparison, in which the primary and secondary subjects are juxtaposed for the sake of noting dissimilarities as well as similarities, is to misconstrue the function of a metaphor. In discursively comparing one subject *with* another, we sacrifice the

---

17. John Whatley, "'Like,'" *Proceedings of the Aristotelian Society* 62 (1961–62), pp. 99–116; A. Bain, *English Composition and Rhetoric* (New York, 1888). Cf. *Models and Metaphors*, p. 36.

*Metaphor*

distinctive power and effectiveness of a good metaphor. The literal comparison lacks the ambience and suggestiveness, and the imposed "view" of the primary subject, upon which a metaphor's power to illuminate depends. In a metaphor as powerful as Pascal's, of man as a "thinking reed" (*un roseau pensant*), the supporting ground is disconcertingly simple, being intended chiefly to highlight human frailty and weakness (*faiblesse*). The figure's effect depends, in this instance, very much on the ambience.

It is helpful to remind oneself that "is like" has many uses, among them: to point to some obvious, striking, or salient resemblance as in, "Doesn't he look like Mussolini?" (where some such qualification as "*looks* like" or "*sounds* like" is needed); in an "open comparison," to mark the start of a detailed, literal point-by-point comparison; or as a mere stylistic variation upon the metaphorical form (which raises nearly all the questions I am here trying to answer).

Thinking in Metaphors

The foregoing account, which treats a metaphor, roughly speaking, as an instrument for drawing implications grounded in perceived analogies of structure between two subjects belonging to different domains, has paid no attention to the state of mind of somebody who *affirms* a metaphorical statement. A good metaphor sometimes *impresses*, strikes, or seizes its producer: We want to say we had a "flash of insight," not merely that we were comparing $A$ with $B$, or even that we were thinking of $A$ as if it were $B$. But to say seriously, emphatically, that, "Life is the receipt and transmission of information," is at least to be thinking of life *as* the passage of information (but not that, merely). Similarly for all metaphorical utterances that are asserted and not merely entertained.

It might, therefore, be a large step forward in becoming clearer about what might be called *metaphorical thought* (a neglected topic of major importance) if we had a better grasp on what it is to think of something ($A$) *as* something else ($B$). What, then, is it to think of $A$ as $B$?

Consider the relatively simple case of thinking of the geo-

*More about Metaphor*

metrical figure sometimes called the "Star of David" in the following different ways:

(1) as an equilateral triangle set upon another of the same size (figure 1);
(2) as a regular hexagon, bearing an equilateral triangle upon each of its edges (figure 2);
(3) as three superimposed congruent parallelograms (figure 3);
(4) as the trace left by a point moving continuously around the perimeter of the Star and then around the interior hexagon;
(5) as in (4), but with the point tracing out the hexagon before moving to the outside.

One might ask a child to think of the figure in each of these ways in turn. In the difficult third case of the three parallelograms, he would probably need some help, so there is something that he can be taught to do. But what?

The images one forms in trying to obey instructions corresponding to these five aspects of the Star are heuristically essential. A slow learner might be helped by having the different geometrical forms outlined in contrasting colors or, in cases (4) and (5), by watching a moving pencil point actually produce the figure. But the comprehension could not consist merely in possessing such images, important as they may be: Any competent teacher would ask the learner such questions as whether the moving point could trace the whole figure continuously—or, in the simpler cases, whether the triangles in question had the same size and shape. A test of mastery is the ability to tease out the implications of the intended perceptual analysis.

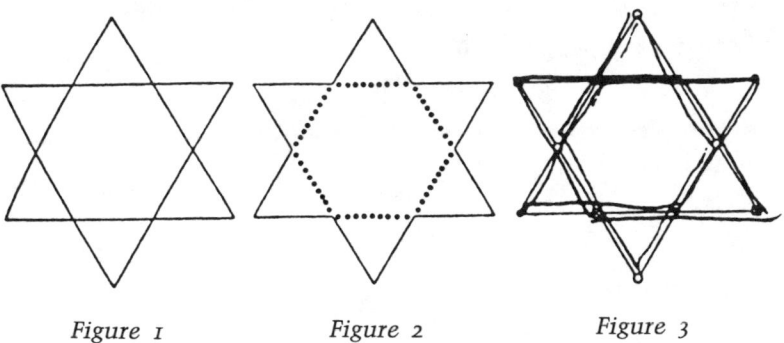

Figure 1      Figure 2      Figure 3

*Metaphor*

So far, the case somewhat resembles what happens when we see some *A* as metaphorically *B*: The child sees the Star *as* superimposed parallelograms; a metaphor thinker sees life *as* a flow of information; both apply concepts that yield discovery; both manifest skills shown in ability to tease out suitable implications of their respective insights. But this comparison is somewhat lame, because the child learner, unlike the metaphor thinker, has not yet been required to make *conceptual innovations*, the parallelograms he perceives being just those he had antecedently learned to draw and recognize.

So let us vary the illustration. One might ask a child to think of each of the following figures as a triangle: one composed of three curved segments; a straight line segment (viewed as a collapsed triangle, with its vertex on the base); two parallel lines issuing from a base segment (with the vertex "gone to infinity"); and so on. The imaginative effort demanded in such exercises (familiar to any student of mathematics) is not a bad model for what is needed in producing, handling, and understanding all but the most trivial of metaphors. That the use of the relevant concepts employed should *change* (so that "game" is *made* to apply to marriage; "information" to life; "reed" to man; and so on) seems essential to the operation.

Why stretch and twist, press and expand, concepts in this way—Why try to see *A* as metaphorically *B*, when it literally is not *B*? Well, because we *can* do so, conceptual boundaries not being rigid, but elastic and permeable; and because we often need to do so, the available literal resources of the language being insufficient to express our sense of the rich correspondences, interrelations, and analogies of domains conventionally separated; and because metaphorical thought and utterance sometimes embody insight expressible in no other fashion.

How Do We Recognize Metaphors?

While praising the interaction theory, Monroe C. Beardsley has urged that it is incomplete in not explaining what it is about the metaphorical attribution that *informs* us that the modifier is metaphorical rather than literal.[18]

Elsewhere, Beardsley states the tasks of a theory of metaphor as follows:

> The problem is to understand how that radical shift of intension [how the metaphorical modifer acquires a special sense in its particular context] comes about; *how we know that the modifier is to be taken metaphorically;* and how we construe or explicate its meaning correctly.[19]

The supplement that Beardsley desires, therefore, seems to be some *diagnostic criterion,* as it might be called, for the occurrence of a metaphorical statement, some mark or indication that will allow its presence and metaphorical character to be detected. I use "diagnostic criterion" here to suggest a bodily symptom, such as a rash, that serves as a reliable sign of some abnormal state though not necessarily qualifying as a defining condition. But Beardsley may, after all, be seeking more ambitiously an observable and *necessary condition* for a statement to be metaphorical.

The need for some such identification criterion, essential or merely diagnostic, has been forcibly urged by other writers. Ina Loewenberg says:

> Any satisfactory formulation of the principle of metaphor requires the identifiability of metaphors since they cannot be understood or produced unless recognized as such.[20]

Here "*the* principle of a metaphor" alludes to her contention that metaphors "exemplify a single principle of semantic change." If

---

18. Monroe C. Beardsley, *Aesthetics: Problems in the Philosophy of Criticism* (New York, 1958), p. 161; italics added.

19. Monroe C. Beardsley, "Metaphor," in *Encyclopedia of Philosophy,* ed. Paul Edwards (New York, 1967), 5:285; italics added.

20. Ina Loewenberg, "Truth and Consequences of Metaphors," *Philosophy and Rhetoric* 6 (1973), pp. 30–46.

"identifiability" is taken in a broad sense, I could agree with Loewenberg's requirement, with a possible reservation about a "producer" being necessarily aware of using a metaphor. But the rest of her valuable essay shows that she, like Beardsley at least part of the time, is demanding what I have called a "diagnostic criterion" for a statement to be metaphorical.

Beardsley proceeds to offer such a diagnostic criterion as the cornerstone of his "controversion theory."[21] According to him, the recognizable mark of a metaphorical statement is that *taken literally* it would have to count as a logical contradiction or an absurdity, in either case something patently *false*.

An obvious objection is that this test, so far as it fits, will apply equally to such other tropes as oxymoron or hyperbole, so that it would at best certify the presence of some figurative statement, but not necessarily a metaphor. A more serious objection is that authentic metaphors need not manifest the invoked controversion, though many of them do. Suppose I counter the conversational remark, "As we know, man is a wolf—*homo homini lupus*," by saying, "Oh, no, man is not a wolf but an ostrich."[22] In context, "Man is not a wolf" is as metaphorical as its opposite, yet it clearly fails the controversion test. The point is easy to generalize: The negation of any metaphorical statement can itself be a metaphorical statement and hence possibly true if taken literally. Nor need the examples be confined to such negatives. When we say, "He does indeed live in a glass house," of a man who actually lives in a house made of glass, nothing prevents us from using the sentence to make a metaphorical statement.

Our recognition of a metaphorical statement depends essentially upon two things: Our general knowledge of what it is to *be*

21. In later writing, he called his view the "Revised Verbal Opposition Theory" (Monroe C. Beardsley, "The Metaphorical Twist," *Philosophy and Phenomenological Research* 22 [1962]). The preferred later title indicates his interest in explaining the supposed "tension between the subject and the modifier by which we are alerted to something special, odd and startling in the combination" (p. 285). Here he has in mind what would be an essential and not merely a diagnostic feature of metaphor.

22. This is an adaptation of an example used by T. Binkley, "On the Truth and Probity of Metaphor," *Journal of Aesthetics and Art Criticism* 33 (1974), pp. 171–80. For many further counterexamples to Beardsley's thesis, see Ted Cohen, "Notes on Metaphor," *Journal of Aesthetics and Art Criticism* 34 (1976), pp. 249–59.

a metaphorical statement, and our specific judgment that a metaphorical reading of a given statement is here preferable to a literal one. The decisive reason for the choice of interpretation may be, as it often is, the patent falsity or incoherence of the literal reading—but it might equally be the banality of that reading's truth, its pointlessness, or its lack of congruence with the surrounding text and nonverbal setting. The situation in cases of doubt as to how a statement is best taken is basically the same as that in other cases of ambiguity. And just as there is no infallible test for resolving ambiguity, so there is none to be expected in discriminating the metaphorical from the literal.

There is an important mistake of method in seeking an infallible mark of the presence of metaphors. The problem seems to me analogous to that of distinguishing a joke from a nonjoke. If a philosopher, whose children have trouble in deciding when he is joking, introduces the convention that a raised thumb indicates seriousness, he might sometimes be joking in raising his thumb! An explicit assertion that a remark is being made metaphorically (perhaps the best candidate for a reliable diagnostic sign) cannot guarantee that a metaphor is in question, for that does not depend simply upon its producer's intentions, and the sign might itself be used metaphorically. Every criterion for a metaphor's presence, however plausible, is defeasible in special circumstances.

If Beardsley and other critics of the interaction view are, after all, not looking for a diagnostic criterion but rather something essential to a metaphor's *being* a metaphor, my above rebuttals will miss their mark. But then the tension of which Beardsley and others speak seems to be only one feature of that peculiar mode of language use in which a metaphor's focus induces a "projection" of a "secondary system," as already explained in this paper. "Tension" seems to me somewhat less suggestive than "interaction," but there is no point in quarreling over labels.


Are Metaphors Ever "Creative"?

The production of a new metaphorical statement obviously introduces some small change into a world that includes statements and the thoughts they express, as well as clouds and rocks.

## Metaphor

Even the reaffirmation of an old metaphor can be viewed as a trivial insertion into the world of a new token of a known statement-type. That metaphors should be creative in this boring way is hardly worth mentioning except for the sake of contrast.

Emphasis upon the alleged creativity of metaphors becomes more interesting when they are viewed as miniature poems or poem fragments. But the production of a work of art would interest me here, given the general thrust of this essay, only if such a work "tells us something about the world." Indeed, I intend to defend the implausible contention that a metaphorical statement can sometimes generate new knowledge and insight by *changing* relationships between the things designated (the principal and subsidiary subjects). To agree would be to assign a strong cognitive function to certain metaphors; but to disagree is not necessarily to relegate them entirely to some realm of fiction.[23] For it may be held that such metaphors reveal connections without *making* them. (Would it not be unsettling to suppose that a metaphor might be self-certifying, by generating the very reality to which it seems to draw attention?)

In my earlier essay, I stated one form of what might be called the "strong creativity thesis" in this way:

> It would be more illuminating in some of these cases [i.e., of metaphors imputing similarities difficult to discern otherwise] to say that the metaphor creates the similarity than to say that it formulates some similarity antecedently existing. (*Metaphor*, p. 37)

It will be noticed that the claim was explicitly hedged: to say "it would be more illuminating" to view some metaphors as ontologically creative falls short of claiming that they are creative. Yet no remark in *Metaphor* has provoked stronger dissent.

---

23. According to M. Oakeshott, *The Voice of Poetry in the Conversation of Mankind* (London, 1959), all "poetic imagining" (as in the use of indispensable metaphors) is concerned with "fiction," which would be radically misconstrued as "contributions to an enquiry into the nature of the real world." He adds: "When it is said that poetic imagining is 'seeing things as they really are' . . . we seem to have been inveigled back into a world composed, not of images but of cows and cornfields" (pp. 45–46). Contrast with this Wallace Stevens' dictum: "Metaphor creates a new reality from which the original appears to be unreal," *Opus Posthumous* (New York, 1957), p. 169.

Khatchadourian, in the course of a generally approving account of the interaction view, thinks the thesis cannot be right. He asks rhetorically, "How can one, anyway, literally create a feature or a similarity by means of a metaphor?" Granting that a metaphor user "can bring into prominence *known* features . . . which he thinks deserve special attention" and thereby "give us a new vision or a new insight," Khatchadourian concludes that "the creation of some effect in the hearer or reader [does not involve] *the creation of a similarity* between the principal and the subsidiary subject."[24]

Long ago, S. J. Brown summarily dismissed a related contention (on the part of Gustave Lanson) that, by means of metaphor, "Our mind, perceiving a common quality in two different objects, or *creating between them a relation which assimilates them to one another*, names one of them by a term which suits, or belongs to, the other." Brown says: "How the mind can create a relation which does not previously exist, M. Lanson does not explain, nor ought such explanation be expected of a writer on literary theory."[25] Such offhand rejection is clearly motivated by a picture of the "relation" in question as being "objective" or "out there"— existing quite as independently as the relation of "having-the-same-height-as": One rightly wants to deny that cubits can be added to stature by saying or thinking so. But this conception of some objective relation as antecedently existing is question-begging when applied to that variegated set of relations that we bundle together as "similarity."[26] When applied to the explication of metaphors, "is like" is not as sharply contrasted with *"looks* like" as "is taller than" is with *"looks* taller than." The imputed relations in a generative metaphor, one might say, must have a subjective as well as an objective aspect, but each may contribute

24. Haig Khatchadourian, "Metaphor," *British Journal of Aesthetics* 8 (1968), pp. 235–36; my italics.
25. Brown, *World of Imagery*, p. 47; my italics.
26. For which see Whatley's illuminating essay "'Like.'" I agree with him that "to say, as philosophers sometimes at least imply, that 'A is like B' designates a 'similarity relation' tends to group like-statements to statements of physical, temporal and other purely objective relationships" (p. 112). On the whole, Whatley tends to stress nonobjective uses of "like"; but he also says of some uses that "there is, in all but peculiar circumstances, some very definite sense in which these resemblances must correspond to fact" (p. 113).

to the other, as I hope to show. I shall try to make the strong creativity thesis at least plausible by considering a series of five answers to questions having the form, "Did *X* exist before it was perceived?"

(1) Did the other side of the moon exist before it was seen?

It would take a fanatical idealist to say no. We think, of course, of the rocks, plains, and mountains as having been there all the time, prior to observation. It is crucial to this conception—as contrasted with some of the following examples—that the existence of the physical objects and configurations in question is held to depend in no way upon the existence of human or other sentient beings, or upon their contingent possession and use of thought and language.

(2) Did genes exist before their existence was recognized by biologists?

The question might be rephrased as, "Did things properly *called* 'genes' exist before they were admitted into accepted biological theory?" An affirmative answer is no doubt used to contrast this case with those in which the "objects" in question were *synthesized* by human agency. *Qua* things found but not made, "natural" and not "artificial," genes—it must be agreed—were "there all the time," even before their existence was discovered. But it is less obvious that *genes* "were there all the time, waiting to be discovered." The term "gene" has its place within a man-made theory, in whose absence it would have no intelligible use: The relation between "gene" and what that term designates is more like that of a dot on a map and the city it represents than like that of a personal name and the person it designates. So the proper answer to this second question should be "Yes and no."

(3) Were there bankrupts before the financial institutions of the Western world were developed?

If the question is taken in a literal sense, the only acceptable answer must be no. For here the allusion to man-made constructions (institutions rather than developed theory) is uncontroversial: "Bankrupt" (applied to someone judged insolvent on petition to a court of law) had no application before the requisite legal procedures had come into existence. A positive answer to the question would need to take the tortuously counterfactual form of: "*If* there had been the corresponding legal institutions (say in 1066), such-and-such a person would have been judged a bankrupt *if* the requisite petitions had been lodged."

(4) Did the view of Mount Everest from a point one hundred feet above its summit exist before anybody had seen that view?

An affirmative answer can be accepted only in the counterfactual sense proposed in the last paragraph: "If anybody had been in a position to view the mountain from the point specified, it *would* have looked as it does now from a plane flying overhead (i.e., the view has not changed)." But if we agree, we should reject the reifying mythology of the *unseen* view, "there all the time" and available for inspection like some ethereal emanation. The notion of a "view" implicates human beings as possible perceivers (though not as the creators and subjects of legal institutions, as in the last case): It is logically necessary that a view can be *seen* (viewed). Now, when a certain view is actually seen, that is a fact about the mountain as well as about the viewer—about a world that includes both. It is objectively true, not a matter of mere convention or whim, that the view of Everest from such-and-such a point has such-and-such features.

(5) Did the slow-motion appearance of a galloping horse exist before the invention of cinematography?

Here the "view" is necessarily mediated by a man-made instrument (though this might cease to be true if some mutant children were born with the power to see "slow motion" with one eye). And yet what is seen in a slow-motion film becomes a part of the world once it is seen.

The last example comes the closest to what I originally had in mind by the strong creativity thesis. If some metaphors are what might be called "cognitive instruments," indispensable for perceiving connections that, once perceived, are *then* truly present, the case for the thesis would be made out. Do metaphors ever function as such cognitive instruments? I believe so. When I first thought of Nixon as "an image surrounding a vacuum," the verbal formulation was necessary to my seeing him in this way. Subsequently, certain kinetic and visual images have come to serve as surrogates for the original verbal formulation, which still controls the sensory imagery and remains available for ready reaffirmation.

For such reasons as this, I still wish to contend that some metaphors enable us to see aspects of reality that the metaphor's production helps to constitute. But that is no longer surprising if one believes that the world is necessarily a world *under a certain description*—or a world seen from a certain perspective. Some metaphors can create such a perspective.

Can a Metaphorical Statement Ever Reveal "How Things Are"?

In the last section, my attention was fixed upon the creative or productive aspects of generative metaphors, in virtue of which they can sometimes function as cognitive instruments through which their users can achieve novel views of a domain of reference. But a view, however mediated, must be a view of *something:* My task here is to make some suggestions about what that "something" is and how far its possession can yield insight about "how things are."

I have chosen the unpretentious formula "how things are" in order to avoid the fixation of a number of writers who discuss the same topic under the rubric, "Can metaphorical statements be *true?*"[27] Their strategy seems to me misguided and liable to in-

27. Unsurprisingly, a notable exception is J. L. Austin, who says: "We become obsessed with 'truth' when discussing statements, just as we become obsessed with 'freedom' when discussing conduct. . . . Not merely is it jejune to suppose that all a statement aims to be is 'true,' but it may further be questioned whether every 'statement' does aim to be true at all. The principle of Logic, that 'Every proposition must be true or false,' has too long operated as the simplest, most persuasive and most pervasive form of the descriptive fallacy": "Truth," in *Philosophical Papers* (Oxford, 1961), pp. 98–99.

duce distortion by focusing exclusively upon that special connection between statement and reality that we signal by the attribution of truth value. In ordinary language, the epithet "true" has more restricted uses than philosophers usually recognize. It is most uncontroversially appropriate in situations where the prime purpose is to state a "fact," that is, where the fact-stating statement in question is associated with some accepted procedure for verification or confirmation: A witness who swears to "tell the truth and nothing but the truth" is expected to "speak plainly," that is, to eschew figurative language, and commits himself not only to refrain from lying, but also to abstain from producing probability statements, generalizations, explanations, and interpretations of actions (though some of these excluded types of statements may in other contexts, for example, those of scientific inquiry, be properly judged true or false). In such fact-stating uses, the concepts of truth and falsity are closely associated with such semantic paronyms as "lying," "believing," "knowing," "evidence," "contradiction," and others. The relevant linguistic subpractice (or *Sprachspiel*, as Wittgenstein would call it) characteristically assumes agreement about ways of checking upon what is being said, and about ways of contesting or qualifying such sayings.

Hence, one way to recognize that we are in *this* domain of language use is to consider whether supplementary questions such as "Are you perhaps lying?"; "What's the evidence?"; "How do you know?"; "Aren't you contradicting what you said a moment ago?"; and the like are in order. With such considerations in mind, we can readily dismiss the question about whether metaphorical statements have truth values. If somebody insists that "Nixon is an image surrounding a vacuum," it would be inept to ask soberly whether the speaker *knew* that to be so, or how he came to know it, or how we could check on the allegation, or whether he was saying something consistent with his previous assertion that Nixon was a shopkeeper. Such supplementary moves are never appropriate to any metaphorical statements except those degenerately "decorative" or expendable ones in which the metaphorical focus can be replaced by some literal equivalent. It is a violation of philosophical grammar to assign either truth or falsity to strong metaphors.

What lies behind the desire to stretch "true" to fit some such cases (as when somebody might quite intelligibly respond to the Nixon-metaphor by saying, "How true!") is a recognition that an emphatic, indispensable metaphor does not belong to the realm of fiction, and is not merely being used, as some writers allege, for some mysterious aesthetic effect, but really does say something (Nixon, if we are not mistaken, *is* indeed what he is metaphorically said to be).

Such recognition of what might be called the representational aspect of a strong metaphor can be accommodated by recalling other familiar devices for representing "how things are" that cannot be assimilated to "statements of fact." Charts and maps, graphs and pictorial diagrams, photographs and "realistic" paintings, and, above all, models are familiar cognitive devices for *showing* "how things are," devices that need not be perceived as mere substitutes for bundles of statement of fact. In such cases we speak of correctness and incorrectness, without needing to rely upon those overworked epithets, "true" and "false."

This is the clue we need in order to do justice to the cognitive, informative, and ontologically illuminating aspects of strong metaphors. I have been presenting in this essay a conception of metaphors which postulates interactions between two systems, grounded in analogies of structure (partly created, partly discovered). The imputed isomorphisms can, as we have seen, be rendered explicit and are then proper subjects for the determination of appropriateness, faithfulness, partiality, superficiality, and the like. Metaphors that survive such critical examination can properly be held to convey, in indispensable fashion, insight into the systems to which they refer. In this way, they can, and sometimes do, generate insight about "how things are" in reality.

# 4

# *How Metaphors Work: A Reply to Donald Davidson*

Perplexities about Metaphors[1]

To be able to produce and understand metaphorical statements is nothing much to boast about: these familiar skills, which children seem to acquire as they learn to talk, are perhaps no more remarkable than our ability to tell and to understand jokes. How odd then that it remains difficult to explain what we do (and should do) in grasping metaphorical statements. In a provocative paper, "What Metaphors Mean,"[2] Donald Davidson has charged many students of metaphor, ancient and modern, with having committed a "central mistake." According to him, there is "error and confusion" in claiming "that a metaphor has, in addition to its literal sense or meaning, another sense or meaning." The guilty include "literary critics like Richards, Empson, and Winters; philosophers from Aristotle to Max Black; psychologists from Freud and earlier to Skinner and later; and linguists from Plato to Uriel Weinreich and George Lakoff." Good company, if

---

Reprinted, by permission, from *On Metaphor*, ed. Sheldon Sacks (Chicago: University of Chicago Press, 1979). Copyright © 1979 by The University of Chicago Press.

1. I shall use "metaphor" throughout this essay as a concise way of referring to metaphorical *statements*.

2. Donald Davidson, "What Metaphors Mean," in *On Metaphor*, ed. Sheldon Sacks (Chicago, 1979). All further references in text.

somewhat mixed. The error to be extirpated is the "idea that a metaphor has a special meaning" (p. 30).

If Davidson is right, much that has been written about metaphor might well be consigned to the flames. Even if he proves to be wrong, his animadversions should provoke further consideration of the still problematic modus operandi of metaphor.

## The Common Sense of Metaphors

Before addressing Davidson's main contentions, I shall list some assertions, all of which I believe to be true, about a paradigmatic instance of metaphorical statement. It will be convenient to use the remark (R) with which Davidson opens his paper: "Metaphor is the dreamwork of language."[3]

I believe that all of the following assertions are true of R and that corresponding assertions would apply to many other metaphorical statements.

1. The *thought* that metaphor is the dreamwork of language (that R, for short) might have occurred to Davidson, and probably did, before he committed it to paper.[4]
    1.1 If this happened, Davidson *affirmed* that R and he did not merely entertain the thought or use R as an example of metaphor.[5]

---

3. The full sentence is: "Metaphor is the dreamwork of language and, like all dreamwork, its interpretation reflects as much on the interpreter as on the originator" (p. 29). I shall use "R" sometimes to refer to Davidson's *remark*, sometimes to refer to the *sentence* he used.

4. This rather obvious point deserves emphasis, since most students of metaphor overemphasize the quasi-performative aspects of metaphorical utterance. The uses of metaphorical statements are not confined to the role they play in communication with others. R, unlike such a clear performative as "I promise . . . ," makes sense in private thought. It would seem to me farfetched to regard such private utterance as a degenerate case of communication, like a chessplayer "playing with himself."

5. Alternatively, one might say that he *committed* himself to R. I use "affirmed" here in a sense sufficiently broad to permit a command or a question to be affirmed, in order not to beg the question whether somebody affirming a metaphor can be making truth-claims.

1.2 Thereby he expressed a distinctive *view* of metaphor, his topic.[6]
1.21 Davidson had won some new *insight* into what metaphor is.
2 When he wrote out R at the start of his paper, he was *making* that remark—and not quoting the sentence or, as some logicians say, "mentioning" it.[7]
2.1 In so doing, he was writing *in earnest*, not joking or pretending or playacting.
2.11 He *meant* what he wrote.[8]
2.2 In making the remark he was saying something, not merely doing something else such as nudging his reader to find similarities between metaphors and dreamwork.[9]
2.3 A reader could understand or misunderstand Davidson's remark.[10]
3 In Davidson's use of R, the word "dreamwork" was being used metaphorically, and the remaining words literally.[11]
3.1 Davidson was not using R as he would have done had he intended R to be taken literally.[12]
4 In making the remark, R, Davidson chose words precisely appropriate to his intention.[13]

---

6. Probably most of those who agree would find it hard to spell out what having a view amounts to.

7. We lack a convenient label for such straightforward, primary uses of language.

8. Or: *intended* that he should be taken as speaking in *propria persona*, straightforwardly (4.1) and seriously.

9. I intend "saying" here to mean much the same as J. L. Austin's "constating," i.e., the presenting of claims that might be disputed (see 6 and 6.1). We shall see that Davidson emphatically disagrees with 2.2.

10. Of course, a promise or a bet can be misunderstood, so accepting 2.3 need not commit one to accepting 2.2.

11. I call these the *focus* and the *frame* of the sentence respectively. See "Metaphor," ch. 3 of my *Models and Metaphors* (Ithaca, N.Y., 1962), p. 28. See also my "More about Metaphor," pp. 47–76 in this volume.

12. If only because R, taken literally, is plainly false, as Davidson points out in similar cases.

13. I am assuming that Davidson, like other careful writers, would not say "Metaphor *is* dreamwork" unless he intended to say just that and not something else. In the propositions 4 and 4.11, I am urging that the categorical use of the copula in a metaphor of the form "A *is* B" serves a distinctive purpose (though, to be sure, a somewhat obscure one). Thus I regard 4.11 as an important weapon against theorists who wish to reduce metaphor to simile or comparison.

*Metaphor*

- 4.1 He said and intended to say that metaphor is the dreamwork of language.
- 4.11 Davidson would not have been satisfied to say instead that metaphor is *like* linguistic dreamwork; or that the one can be *compared* to the other; or that in metaphorizing[14] we are regarding one thing *as if* it were another.
  - 5 In affirming R, Davidson was implying and intimating various unstated remarks.[15]
  - 5.1 He was implying, but not explicitly saying, that metaphor and dreamwork have some similar or analogous properties.[16]
  - 5.2 He was using "dreamwork" to *allude* to certain Freudian doctrines.[17]
  - 5.3 Davidson was *suggesting* various unstated contentions, left to the reader to develop at discretion, for example, that a metaphor has a latent as well as a manifest content.
  - 5.4 He might reasonably be taken to be suggesting also various *evaluations* of metaphor consonant with the parallel Freudian doctrines about dreams.
    - 6 A reader could *disagree* with Davidson's remark (e.g., by objecting that the underlying analogy was "too thin"—or by saying "Metaphor is sometimes *waking* work").[18]
    - 6.1 Reasons could be offered for and against R.[19]
      - 7 R, or any other metaphorical remark, might be criticized as inept, misleading, obscure, unilluminating, and so forth.[20]

---

14. I shall use this word to refer both to the production of metaphorical statement (whether in thought, speech, or writing) and also to the comprehension of another person's metaphor.

15. It would be arbitrary to restrict a metaphor's content to what is *explicitly* expressed by it. I take the metaphor's author to be committed (4.11) to its implications.

16. It is tempting to say that R implies that metaphor is *like* dreamwork. But the latter assertion implies that metaphor is *not* dreamwork! Only different things can be sensibly compared.

17. Here and in 5.3 I am trying to acknowledge, however inadequately, the aspects of a metaphor's working that cannot plausibly be subsumed under implicit *"saying."*

18. Thus using one metaphor to oppose another, as can sometimes happen.

19. The truth of this and the preceding assertion, 6, supports my own view that metaphors can imply truth-claims (see 2.2).

20. I shall not discuss here the vexed question whether metaphors can be true or false.

7.1 A metaphorical statement, such as R, can fail or succeed.[21]

*Summary:* A metaphorical statement, such as R, can be affirmed (1.1) in private thought (1) and hence need not be addressed to another person. In either case the statement expresses a view of its topic (1.2) and some putative insight (1.21). When a statement is seriously communicated (2, 2.1), its user, if expressing himself precisely, means just what he says or writes (2.11). The author of a metaphor *says* something (2.2), although he will also typically be alluding to (5.1), suggesting (5.3), and evaluating (5.4) other things. When a statement is metaphorical, the sentence used, part only of which consists of a word or words used metaphorically (3), is not intended to be taken literally (3.1). In appropriate and precise formulation, a metaphorical statement cannot be replaced by literal statements of resemblance or comparison, or by allied *as-if* statements (4.11, 2.2), but will usually imply these and other unstated implications (5, 5.1). Metaphors can be understood or misunderstood (2.3) and can be rejected or endorsed (6.1). Metaphorizing may fail or succeed (7.1).

In thus setting out the common sense of the production and understanding of metaphorical remarks, I have abstained from using the verb "to mean" except in one instance (2.11) where it can be replaced. Yet, it would be natural to add further comments about what Davidson *meant* by his metaphorical remark and what he would properly be taken by a competent reader as intending to mean. At a pretheoretical commonsensical level, one would suppose that Davidson could hardly have thought R (1) without meaning something by the words that occurred to him, and it is hard to understand how he could have affirmed R (1.1) unless he meant something by that remark (2.11). Nor could he have acquired insight into the nature of metaphor (1.2 and 1.21) otherwise. I have also claimed that he was *saying* various things, many of them implicitly (2.2, 4.1, 5, and 5.1).

---

21. Anybody inclined to agree with Davidson that "there are no unsuccessful metaphors" (p. 29) might be asked to consider Hegel's metaphor of the solar system as a syllogism whose three terms are the sun, the planets, and the comets (from Julien Benda, *Du style d'idées* [Paris, 1948], p. 143).

## Metaphor

The propositions I have formulated concerning a reader's ability to disagree with $R$ (6) and to offer reasons for such disagreement (6.1) further strengthen the case for thinking that the producer of a metaphor such as $R$ is usually making some *assertions*. Davidson denies this. But it is time to see precisely what he is claiming.

### Davidson's Contentions

A careful reading of Davidson's essay will show that he is concerned to argue three main propositions, the first two of which reject a crucial part of what I have called the "common sense" of metaphor, while the third states his own position.

(A) The producer of a metaphorical statement says nothing more than what is meant when the sentence he uses is taken literally.
(B) The sentence used in making a metaphorical statement has in context nothing more than its literal meaning.[22]
(C) A metaphor producer is drawing attention to a resemblance between two or more things.[23]

---

22. I have expressed these propositions in my own words. Davidson's most explicit statement of his own view is: "A metaphor doesn't say anything beyond its literal meaning (nor does its maker say anything, in using the metaphor, beyond the literal)" (p. 30). Also: "Metaphor runs on the same familiar linguistic tracks that the plainest sentences do" (p. 41).
23. "A metaphor makes us attend to some likeness, often a novel or surprising likeness, between two or more things" (p. 31). Davidson also says, more picturesquely, that a metaphor "nudges us into noting" a likeness which it "intimates" (p. 36); it "invites" us to make comparisons (p. 38); a metaphor "inspires or prompts [an] insight" (p. 45). I suppose it is the metaphor maker who literally invites, prompts, provokes, or nudges the receiver. "A simile tells us, in part, what a metaphor merely nudges us into noting" (p. 36). As for what a simile tells us, "In the case of simile, we note what it literally says, that two things resemble one another; we then regard the objects and consider what similarity would, in the context, be to the point" (p. 38). Davidson here, and throughout, apparently overlooks the fact that a simile can be *figurative*. Thinking of a similarity as a literal statement of mutual resemblance between two things will fail to explain why many similes are not immediately reversible. In ordinary usage, "An atom is like a solar system" does not always imply that "a solar system is like an atom."

## Some Comments on These Contentions

*On (A):* Davidson uses "says" throughout in a more restricted way than would fit my own usage of "affirmed" (for which see n. 5). He would of course not deny that a metaphor producer "says," or perhaps even "affirms," something in the weak sense of uttering the words in question seriously. What he does emphatically wish to deny is that in such utterances any *truth-claims* are made. Sometimes he makes this point by denying that a metaphorical statement has "a specific cognitive content," one that "its author wishes to convey and that the interpreter must grasp if he is to get the message" (p. 44). Anyone who "attempts to state the message, is then fundamentally confused . . . because no such message exists" (p. 45). If such a message were "said" or asserted by the author, his words would have to be taken as "standing for, or expressing, [some alleged] fact" (p. 44). If we are led by a metaphor to appreciate some fact, as may happen, that is because the metaphor works like "a picture or a bump on the head." In Davidson's usage, then, to "say" something metaphorically would be to express some supposed *fact* or facts; the theory that a metaphor ever does so is just "false" (p. 44).

One might suppose that since Davidson regards the sentence used in a metaphorical statement as preserving its ordinary literal meaning, he might take its user to be asserting at least one supposed fact—in our prime example, the alleged fact that metaphor is literally dreamwork. But of course there is no such fact, as Davidson himself emphasizes, "For a metaphor *says* only what shows on its face—usually a patent falsehood or an absurd truth . . . given in the literal meaning of the words" (p. 41): what metaphorical statements, taken literally, assert is nearly always plainly false and absurd. Thus, (A) should be understood to mean that a metaphor producer is "saying" *nothing at all.* What, then, is a metaphor producer doing? We shall see when we come to examine (C).

*On (B):* Davidson devotes much of his paper to attacking the view, supposedly held by contemporary theorists, that some of the words used in a metaphorical remark change their senses when so used. He says that the "central mistake" is "the idea that a metaphor has, in addition to its literal sense or meaning, another sense or meaning" (p. 30). He denies vigorously that in the metaphor "the Spirit of God moved upon the face of the waters" it is proper to "regard the word 'face' as having *an extended meaning*" (p. 32, my italics). He thinks that "according to [the current and erroneous] theory a word has a *new meaning* in a metaphorical context" (p. 35, my italics) and adds, provokingly, "the occasion of the metaphor would, therefore, be the occasion for learning the new meaning." In comparing and contrasting metaphors and lies, he claims that "the difference . . . is not a difference in the words used or what they mean (*in any strict sense of meaning*) but in how the words are used" (p. 41, my italics).[24]

Much of this vigorous polemic is beside the point. I know of no theorist who claims that the words used in metaphorical remarks thereby acquire some new meaning in what Davidson calls, as we have seen, the "only strict sense of meaning."[25] I would guess that the strict sense he has in mind is the "Literal meaning . . . [that] can be assigned to words and sentences apart from particular contexts of use" (p. 31). Well, certainly, when Wallace Stevens called a poem a pheasant, he was not permanently changing the standard dictionary sense of "pheasant," a feat almost never accomplished by a single use of a familiar word. One may indeed agree with Davidson that awareness of the "ordinary

---

24. Davidson does, however, agree with Paul Henle, Nelson Goodman, "and the rest in their accounts of what metaphor accomplishes, except that I think it accomplishes more and that what is additional is different in kind [from meaning anything or saying anything]" (p. 31). I shall examine what Davidson thinks a metaphor "accomplishes" in my comments on proposition (C) below. He is, by the way, mistaken in saddling the writers under attack with thinking of "metaphor as primarily a vehicle for conveying ideas, even if unusual ones" (p. 30). Aristotle et al. can answer for themselves; but no moderately attentive reader of my own writings on metaphor could suppose that I ever maintained that metaphorical statements are *primarily* used "for conveying ideas." I have argued merely that such statements can and usually do have a "cognitive content," or do "carry a message," by virtue of implying assertions with truth-value. Like all of Davidson's opponents, I have stressed that much more than the expression of propositional truth is at work in metaphorical discourse.

25. Webster gives four main senses of "mean"; I wonder how many of these Davidson would regard as "strict"? Alas for Ogden and Richards' efforts to display the endemic ambiguities of the word.

[literal] meaning"[26] is necessary if the metaphor is to be recognized and understood.

The question to be considered, then, is not the idle one of whether the words used in a metaphorical remark astonishingly acquire some permanently new sense but rather the question whether the metaphor maker is *attaching* an altered sense to the words he is using in context. Did Stevens mean by "pheasant" something having a tail and able to fly, thereby committing himself to the absurd idea that a poem literally is a bird? Or was he rather using his remark to *say* something about poetry (the question addressed in proposition (B) above)?

The use of a sentence having a familiar standard sense or meaning in order to say something unusual is too familiar to arouse perplexity. When a chess master says, while watching a match, "No pie from that flour"—or rather makes the corresponding Russian remark[27]—what he means could be of no interest to a baker. So, *pace* Davidson, I see no reason on general grounds to be suspicious of the claim that metaphor makers are indeed saying various things, without thereby inducing any permanent change in the standard meaning of the words used metaphorically.

*On (C):* A sympathetic interpretation of Davidson's positive conception of how metaphors work would be to regard him as supporting the view, advanced by some other writers,[28] that anybody making a metaphorical remark is performing a distinctive speech-act, whose force could be more perspicuously expressed by some such formula as "I (hereby) draw your attention to a likeness between (say) metaphor and dreamwork." I think he might accept this, or something like this, given his reiterated emphasis on how a metaphor producer is *using* words to "nudge,"

---

26. "The ordinary meaning [of a metaphor] in the context of use is odd enough to prompt us to disregard the question of literal truth" (p. 40).

27. "No pie from that flour!" (nothing will come of it) was Tal's comment after the fourth game of the Karpov–Korchnoi match in Baguio apropos of Karpov's use of a dubious opening variation (*Chess Life and Review*, January 1979, p. 44).

28. See, for instance, Dorothy Mack, "Metaphoring as Speech Act," *Poetics* 4 (1975), pp. 211–56; and Ina Loewenberg, "Identifying Metaphors," *Foundations of Language* 12 (1975), pp. 315–38. Ted Cohen's "Metaphor and the Cultivation of Intimacy," in Sacks, *On Metaphor*, might also be read as sympathetic to this approach.

## Metaphor

"intimate," "provoke," and so on rather than to say anything. To be sure, Davidson's many remarks about the *effects* of a metaphor (acting like "a bump on the head") might suggest that he is more interested in what Austin would have called the perlocutionary effects of metaphorical discourse than in any postulated illocutionary force of metaphorical utterance. Either way, there are serious objections.

1. On the speech-act approach, it is hard to make sense of what happens when somebody expresses a thought *to himself* (see proposition 1 in my list of commonsensical truths about metaphor, above). Any clear cases of speech-acts that come readily to mind involve communication with an audience: it makes little sense to think of promising *oneself* something, or warning, advising, pronouncing judgment, and so on, to oneself. What then, on Davidson's view is a soliloquizing thinker, using metaphorical language, supposed to be doing? Nudging and provoking himself to pay attention to some covert likeness? But surely he has already done so? What then is the point of saying to himself that metaphor is dreamwork? Is he perhaps pretending to talk to himself, as if he had not already been seized by an unobvious resemblance between the two things in question?
2. There seems, in Davidson's view, just as little point also in drawing *another* person's attention to a likeness between two things, since, according to him, "all similes are true . . . because everything is like everything" (p. 39). If the hearer agrees with Davidson that "all similes are trivially true" (p. 40), how is he supposed to be prodded by Davidson's dreamwork remark? Is he to attend to the "trivial" similarity between the two things mentioned?
3. If Davidson's view were correct, there would be a readily available and more perspicuous way of expressing a metaphorical thought, whether to oneself or to another person, which would bypass the difficulties listed above that attend any commitment to metaphorizing as speech-act. Why not simply say "Metaphor *is like* dreamwork"? Given that the two things mentioned do not, at first blush, look very much alike, such a remark should do all the nudging, provoking, and intimating that Davidson attributes to the usual metaphorical form. If so, we shall have to explain why all of us have an inveterate and, as I think, justified impulse to say in such cases that A *is* B and not merely that A *is*

*How Metaphors Work*

*like* B (see propositions 4.1 and 4.11 above). The only plausible reply that occurs to me would be to assimilate metaphor to hyperbole (as in "There are hundreds of cats in the garden")—as an exaggerated and somewhat hysterical style of talk to be eschewed by careful thinkers.

4. I believe, therefore, that Davidson's position reduces to a reformulation of the ancient and, as one might have hoped, discredited theory that I have in the past called a "comparison view."[29] I still think that my earlier conclusion that "a comparison view . . . suffers from a vagueness that borders on vacuity"[30] holds against any such view and specifically against Davidson's latest, though unacknowledged, espousal of it.[31]

5. The gravest objection to Davidson's vigorously argued standpoint then is that, while rejecting current views, it supplies no insight into how metaphors work and fails to explain why the use of metaphors seems to so many students of metaphor an indispensable resource.

## The Case against Assigning Meaning to Metaphors

I have been arguing in the last section that Davidson's view of how metaphors work is not as he seems to think a new and illuminating view of the topic but is rather, if I am not mistaken, one that treats metaphors as perversely cryptic substitutes for literal similes. I have claimed that this way of looking at metaphors does not explain how strong metaphors work to express and promote insight. Now somebody who is more sympathetic to Davidson's position than I am might retort that the alternative current views are in no better shape. It seems advisable, therefore, to complete this examination of Davidson's paper by evaluating

29. See my "Metaphor," in *Models and Metaphors*, pp. 35–37, where citations from earlier defenders of such a view are supplied.
30. Ibid., p. 37.
31. Davidson echoes my older criticisms of the view that "equates the figurative meaning of the metaphor with the literal meaning of a simile" when he says that the literal meaning is "usually a painfully trivial simile . . . trivial because everything is like everything, and in endless ways" (p. 37). He doesn't seem to notice that the objection applies equally to his own position, even if one continues to insist that a metaphor does not *say* anything but rather provokes and intimates, etc., something like the perception of symmetrical similarities.

87

his specific objections to what might be called, for short, any *semantic* interpretation of metaphor (of which my "interaction view" would be a special case).

So far as I can see, Davidson presents five objections, reproduced below with a brief reply appended to each.

*First objection:* There are no instructions for devising metaphors; there is no manual for determining what a metaphor 'means' or 'says'; there is no test for metaphor that does not call for taste" (p. 29).

*First reply:* That the meaning of a live or active metaphor cannot count as part of its standard meaning, and is therefore to be found neither in dictionaries or encyclopedias, is a point that has often been made by students of metaphor. Thus I have said in the past that the producer of such a metaphor "is employing conventional means to produce a nonstandard effect, while using only the standard syntactic and semantic resources of his speech community. Yet the meaning of an interesting metaphor is typically new or 'creative', *not inferrible from the standard lexicon*."[32] This point leaves untouched the contention at issue, that a metaphor *producer* means something, possibly novel, by his metaphorical statement.

*Second objection:* "It is no help in explaining how words work in metaphor to posit metaphorical or figurative meanings" (p. 31). Davidson contends that "simply to lodge [the] meaning in the metaphor is like explaining why a pill puts you to sleep by saying it has a dormitive power" (p. 31). He contrasts such pseudoexplanation with the "genuine explanatory power" of an appeal to "literal meaning and literal truth conditions [that] can be assigned to words and sentences apart from particular contexts of use" (p. 31).

*Second reply:* One must agree that it would be pointless and obfuscating to invoke some ad hoc "figurative" sense, not otherwise specified, to explain "how metaphor works its wonders" (p. 31). Nevertheless, it would help us to understand how a particular metaphorical utterance works in its context if we could satisfy ourselves that the *speaker* is then attaching a special extended

---

32. "More about Metaphor"; italics added.

*How Metaphors Work*

sense to the metaphorical "focus" (selecting, as I have explained elsewhere, some of the commonplaces normally associated with his secondary subject, in order to express insight into his primary subject). This view is not open to the charge of invoking fictitious entities.

We may compare explanations of ironic talk: it really does help us to understand what somebody means by saying of a colleague's contribution to a college meeting, "X is so *amusing!*" to realize, as we immediately do, that "amusing" here has a sense contrary to its standard sense. Throughout his essay Davidson seems fixated on the explanatory power of standard sense; but when such an explanation is plainly defective, there can be no objection in principle to invoking what the speaker means when speaking metaphorically.

*Third objection:* The view "that in metaphor certain words take on new, or what are often called 'extended,' meanings [as when somebody calls Tolstoy an infant] . . . cannot, at any rate, be complete," for if in such a context the word "infant" applies correctly to the adult Tolstoy, then "Tolstoy literally was an infant, and all sense of metaphor evaporates" (p. 32).

*Third reply:* Recognition of an "extended" nonce meaning is not intended to be a "complete" explanation of how metaphor works. There is no implied claim, either, that in such use a word "applies correctly." If Davidson's objection were sound, then to perceive that an ironical speaker meant by "amusing" something like "unfunny" would be to make all sense of irony "evaporate." Irony remains irony, even when understood; and so does metaphor.

*Fourth objection:* "If a metaphor has a special cognitive content, why should it be so difficult or impossible to set it out?" (p. 42). Davidson challenges my old contention that a literal paraphrase "inevitably says too much—and with the wrong emphasis."[33] "Why," he asks, "inevitably? Can't we, if we are clever enough, come as close as we please?" (p. 42).

*Fourth reply:* Why not, if we are clear about coming "close" and do not mistake an explication for a translation? I supplied a

---

33. "Metaphor," in *Models and Metaphors*, p. 46.

partial answer to Davidson in the passage preceding the one that he reproduces: "the set of literal statements so obtained will not have the same power to inform and enlighten as the original. For one thing, the implications previously left to a suitable reader to educe for himself, with a nice feeling for their relative priorities and degrees of importance, are now presented explicitly as having equal weight."[34] I went on to say that explication or elaboration of a metaphor's grounds (such as I later supplied in "More about Metaphor," using the example of "Marriage is a zero-sum game") can be extremely valuable "if not regarded as an adequate cognitive substitute for the original."

The point is of general application. Toynbee's remark, in connection with American nuclear policy: "No annihilation without representation," could no doubt be spelled out to render his allusion to the familiar slogan boringly explicit. I suppose any sensitive reader would feel that something of the force and point of the original remark would then have been lost. As in aposiopesis, a metaphor leaves a good deal to be supplied at the reader's discretion. To say something with suggestive indefiniteness is not to say nothing.

*Fifth objection:* "Much of what we are caused to notice [by a metaphor] is not propositional in character" (p. 44).

*Fifth reply:* Agreed. But it is going too far to claim that in understanding a metaphor "What we notice or see is not, *in general*, propositional in character" (p. 45, my italics). A metaphor may indeed convey a "vision" or a "view," as Davidson says, but this is compatible with its also saying things that are correct or incorrect, illuminating or misleading, and so on.

Verdict

If a "semantic" conception of metaphor is open to no more serious objections than those advanced by Davidson (lack of recipes for producing metaphors, absence of explanatory power in the theory, incompleteness of the semantic view, difficulty of para-

---

34. Ibid.

phrasing a metaphor's cognitive content, presence of nonpropositional insight in metaphorical thought), its advocates have no cause for alarm and may rest unabashed in their imputed "error and confusion." The verdict must be "nonproven."

In my opinion, the chief weakness of the "interaction" theory, which I still regard as better than its alternatives, is lack of clarification of what it means to say that in a metaphor one thing is thought of (or viewed) as another thing. Here, if I am not mistaken, is to be found a prime reason why unregenerate users of appropriate metaphors may properly reject any view that seeks to reduce metaphors to literal statements of the comparisons or the structural analogies which *ground* the metaphorical insight. To think of God *as* love and to take the further step of identifying the two is emphatically to do something more than to *compare* them as merely being alike in certain respects. But what that "something more" is remains tantalizingly elusive: we lack an adequate account of metaphorical thought.[35]

35. I have made some preliminary suggestions in the section "Thinking in Metaphors" of "More about Metaphor."

# RATIONALITY

# 5

## *Ambiguities of Rationality*

> *What is the answer? [and after a pause] but then what is the question?*
> —Gertrude Stein's last words

The Fundamental Question

In the Platonic dialogue *Phaedrus*, Socrates is made to say, at the outset of a discussion about love:

> [I]f anyone wants to deliberate successfully about anything, there is one thing he must do at the outset: he must know what he is deliberating about; otherwise he is bound to go utterly astray. Now most people fail to realize that they don't know what this or that really is; consequently, when they start discussing something, they dispense with an agreed definition, assuming that they know the thing; later on they naturally find, to their cost, that they agree neither with each other nor with themselves.[1]

I take Socrates to be asking for an initial definition of love. Accepting his sensible admonition at least provisionally, I propose that we try to agree on a preliminary definition of rationality; but

Reprinted, by permission, from *Naturalism and Rationality*, ed. Newton Garver and Peter H. Hare (Buffalo: Prometheus Books, 1986).
  1. Plato, *Phaedrus*, trans. R. Hackforth (Cambridge, 1972), 237b–d.

this will prove harder than might be initially expected. For one might hope that a preliminary definition would omit any question-begging *doctrine* about the definiendum and this proves to be a difficult task.

Socrates' own account of "what he is deliberating about" illustrates the difficulty of excluding premature doctrine. He says that we "all see that love is an irrational desire which overcomes the tendency of opinion towards right, and is led away to the enjoyment of beauty and especially personal beauty."[2] Is this an account of what we *mean* by love—or is it a debatable doctrine about love? Is it absurd to say that Socrates' friends loved an ugly man? I think that Socrates was not providing a definition of "love," but was rather offering a mistaken account of the nature of love.

## Moore's Procedure

My quotation from the *Phaedrus* might well remind us of the famous opening sentence of G. E. Moore's *Principia Ethica*. Moore starts by saying that differences and disagreements in ethics "*as in all philosophical studies* [my italics] are mainly due to a very simple cause: namely to the attempt to answer questions without first discovering precisely *what* question you desire to answer." This implies that we should start by defining the target of the philosophical inquiry. But Moore's subsequent discussion leads him in fact no further than distinguishing the quality of goodness from a determination of the extension of that quality (i.e., to a determination of the things that *are* good).

If we were to use Moore's famous technique of the "open question" in our present search for a definition of rationality, we might well end with the unilluminating and somewhat embarrassing conclusion that rationality is just rationality "and no other thing"—and thus be led to conclude that rationality is indefinable. But the open question argument has been sufficiently

---

2. *The Works of Plato*, trans. Benjamin Jowett (New York, 1965), p. 393.

discredited by subsequent criticism.³ Whatever we think of Moore's view that goodness is indefinable because it is a simple quality, it is surely evident that rationality, at any rate, is complex, and hence amenable in principle to the kind of analytic definition that Moore sought.

Philosophers, economists, social scientists, and many other scholars have indeed been lavish in supplying, often with striking assurance, mutually conflicting definitions of rationality. It seems that those who have most earnestly meditated on the nature of rationality cannot even agree at the outset about "what we are deliberating about" under the elusive label of 'rationality'.

Russell's Definition

Bertrand Russell once said, with customary dogmatism:

> 'Reason' has a perfectly clear and precise meaning. It signifies the choice of the right means for the end that you wish to achieve. It has nothing whatever to do with the choice of ends.⁴

(I shall not distinguish for the present between 'Reason' and 'rationality'.)

This conception, which is often called one of *instrumental* rationality, continues to be extraordinarily influential. It is, for instance, an important assumption of widely accepted models of Bayesian choice theory.⁵

No matter what Russell says, we can and should deliberate rationally about "ends." This is so, even when the ends in question are desires (traditionally, one of the limits for the applicability of rational considerations). Consider the kind of case dis-

---

3. See Arthur N. Prior, *Logic and the Basis of Ethics* (Oxford, 1949) and the important earlier work by W. K. Frankena, "The Naturalistic Fallacy," *Mind* (1939), pp. 472ff.

4. Bertrand Russell, Preface to *Human Society in Ethics and Politics* (London, 1954).

5. See my discussion and criticism of the Bayesian model in "Making Intelligent Choices: How Useful Is Decision Theory?" *Dialectica* 39 (1985), pp. 19–34.

cussed by J. D. Mabbott.[6] I have two desires, say to go swimming and to continue to work on this essay. Reflection that I can swim only if I go now may properly lead to the postponement of gratification of the second desire, *even if that desire is the stronger* (i.e., if I would rather write than swim if I were forced to choose between them). This important type of *management of desires*, as it might be called, demands and can receive rational deliberation. (In such cases, as Mabbott says, Reason can no longer be plausibly regarded as the mere "slave of the passions.")

Oakeshott's Definition

In an essay entitled "Rational Conduct," Michael Oakeshott, in sharp opposition to Russell, vigorously objects to any kind of recommended conduct "in which an independently premeditated end is pursued and which is determined solely by that end."[7] His own substitute for the instrumental conception runs as follows:

> [T]he only significant way of using the word "rational" [a charming counterecho of Russell's dogmatism about the meaning of 'Reason'] is when we mean to indicate . . . *faithfulness to the knowledge of how to conduct the activity we are engaged in.*" (P. 20, italics in the original text)

More succinctly, "practical human conduct may be counted 'rational' in respect to its faithfulness to a knowledge of how to behave well" (p. 26). A conception surely too vague and broad to be useful.

Human Beings as Preeminently Rational

Many of the available and mutually conflicting conceptions of Reason are motivated by the ancient and still influential notion

6. J. D. Mabbott, "Reason and Desire," in *Education and the Development of Reason*, ed. R. F. Dearden et al. (London, 1972), pp. 320–31.
7. Michael Oakeshott, "Rational Conduct," *Cambridge Journal* 4 (1950), p. 5.

that, as Locke puts it, "the word reason . . . stands for a faculty in man, that faculty whereby man is supposed to be distinguished from beasts, and wherein it is evident that he much surpasses them."[8] Darwin said that "of all the faculties of the human mind, it will be admitted that Reason stands at the summit."[9]

This may well be doubted, however. The Earl of Rochester, for one, called Reason "an *ignis fatuus* of the mind" (A Satire Against Mankind), and said he would "rather be a dog, a monkey, or a bear, Or anything but that vain animal who is so proud of being rational."

Gilbert Ryle identified the rationality involved in the ancient view that man is essentially a rational animal with our power of exercising "Thought." He found Thought "in the most hospitable sense of the word" involved in such distinctively human activities as playing games, seeing jokes, striking bargains—and even feeling impatience or irritation.[10]

In a similar vein, Richard Robinson has claimed that "the word reason is our name for the ideal of thinking."[11] Nothing in Ryle and Robinson's conceptions excludes the possibility, *pace* Russell, of using reason to think about the choice of *ends*.

Such examples of rampant disagreement could easily be multiplied. It would not be unfair to conclude that the above cited dicta show their authors to be using the key word in different, if possibly related, senses.

In actual usage by philosophers and other scholars, 'Rationality' is a concertina word, sometimes swelling, in a "hospitable spirit," to extravagant extension, but at other times contracting to implausibly narrowed stipulations. The concept of rationality, one might say, is *incorrigibly elusive*.

---

8. John Locke, *Essay Concerning Human Understanding*, ed. A. C. Fraser (Oxford, 1894), 2:386. Locke says that "the word *reason* in the English language has many different significations" and his editor, Fraser, comments that *Reason* is "among the most ambiguous of philosophical terms." He takes Locke to be using it as "synonymous with *reasoning*" (p. 384).
9. Charles Darwin, *Descent of Man* (London, 1871), 1:46.
10. Gilbert Ryle, "A Rational Animal," reprinted in his *Collected Papers* (London, 1971), 2:419.
11. Richard Robinson, *An Atheist's Values* (Oxford, 1964), p. 105.

*Rationality*

## Why So Much Disagreement?

We cannot afford to be complacent about such radical disagreements in analytical definitions of rationality. The targets of the incorrigibly elusive concepts of rationality and its semantic associates are important. Even if we resorted to the drastic remedy of a temporary or permanent ban on the use of the label, we would still need to discuss the benefits and limitations of what we applaud as "rational" or stigmatize as "irrational." But before discussing what might be done to improve the relevant philosophical investigations, it might be helpful to diagnose some of the main reasons for modern and ancient disagreements about "what we are talking about." I would like to suggest the following explanations.

1. 'Rationality' and its associate 'Reason' (with a capital R) refer to highly complex matters. It is suggestive to recall that Aristotle and other Attic thinkers had no single word or phrase equivalent to our 'rational' or 'rationality'. Thus Aristotle frequently uses the three words, *nous*, *logos*, and *dianoia*, in discussing rationality. (Apparently Cicero introduced the comprehensive label *ratio* much later.) We might profitably follow Aristotle's practice, by separately identifying related but distinguishable aspects of what is involved in approvably "rational" choice, belief, and attitude.

2. 'Reason' and 'reason' suffer from belonging to the untechnical vocabulary of nonprofessionals. But men or women "in the street" would find it very hard to say what they mean by 'reason'. The would-be precise and technical label of 'rationality', contaminated by its origin in common usage, tends accordingly to be ill defined. Because insufficiently technical in actual use, 'rational' and 'rationality' are prone to unnoticed distortion, a hazard that does not arise in such well-defined scientific terms as, say, 'entropy' or such patently technical philosophical terms as 'opaque reference'.

3. Since 'rational', in both common and philosophical usage, is and is usually intended to be a *laudatory* epithet (although there are striking exceptions even to this), there is a standing temptation to incorporate the investigator's normative ideals in its meaning. But questions about whether rationality is (always? sometimes?)

a good thing ought surely not to be begged by definitions embodying the analyst's unargued value judgments.

4. Ancient and modern conceptions of the nature of rationality and the role of Reason tend to be distressingly inadequate to the roles of intelligent thought and deliberation in "rational" choices between available alternatives. For the classical conception of Reason as a special "faculty" that controls the otherwise unbridled forces of "passions" (or, in Hume's famous *volte face*, acts as the "slave" of such irrational influences) clearly will not do. I would suppose it sufficiently obvious that application of active intelligence should itself be regarded as motivated by a "passion"; and the mythology of independent "faculties" has long ago been abandoned by professional psychologists. In the absence of agreed and thoroughly tested views about how our minds work in making choices or in arriving at beliefs, philosophical views about the nature of rationality are apt to remain unsatisfyingly primitive.

5. The theory of definition implicit in the views of most scholars who have discussed the "nature of rationality" usually conforms to the Aristotelian or Linnean scheme of definition by classification and division (*per genus et differentiam*). But even the first step, of determining "what kind of a thing" rationality is, presents formidable difficulties, as anybody who tries to answer that question will be able to confirm.

## Starting from Examples

In trying to articulate such complex, though familiar, concepts as 'cause' or 'knowledge' or the other concepts that continue to engage the best efforts of philosophers, I have often found it helpful to start from "paradigm cases" of the correct use of the concept-label.[12] For instance: in searching for a paradigm case of the application of, say, '(logically) valid', I would start by considering an exemplary argument that would generally be agreed to be unquestionably valid, "if anything is." Then, if all goes well, one can proceed to look for the criteria that we actually use in recog-

---

12. For some appeals to paradigm cases, see for instance, my "Making Something Happen," in *Models and Metaphors* (Ithaca, N.Y., 1962), or "Reasonableness," in *The Prevalence of Humbug* (Ithaca, N.Y., 1983).

nizing the paradigm instance as an unquestionable case of correct application of the concept in question.

However, I have found it surprisingly hard to find a paradigm case of rational choice. On the other hand, it is somewhat easier to find a case of *irrational* choice. (Consider, for instance, the case of a child who eats some spinach "because I *hate* the taste of it." Even that episode, however, might be explained as an attempt to annoy a parent or a perverse desire for self-mortification!) I am tempted to think that, in J. L. Austin's phrase, it is 'irrational' rather than 'rational' "that wears the trousers." But surely there is more to rationality than the absence of irrationality. Given the difficulty of finding unproblematic paradigm cases of rational conduct, I have therefore preferred, in the present inquiry, to report some selected judgments of rationality by educated respondents.

A Preliminary Survey of Usage

Some years ago, while helping to conduct a seminar on rationality and related topics for graduate students at Oxford, I distributed a questionnaire. (It is reproduced as an appendix to this essay.) Some philosophical friends who had heard of my experiment obtained permission to distribute the same questionnaire at the University of Durham (circulated among faculty members) and at York University, Toronto (in a large introductory course in government).

The reader will notice that those answering the questionnaire were offered two ways of evading the application of "rational," "irrational," or "neither" (see the instructions for saying "can't answer" [option C] or "undecided how to answer" [option U]. The participants were also invited to comment on the questions and were urged to work on the questionnaire at leisure.

On examining the results, my first surprise was to find that very few of the respondents used the evasive responses (though one humorist did write "C" for each of the twenty items!).

In summarizing the results, I treated the responses to a given item as if they constituted an election of one of the most appropriate answers. Thus, at Oxford, with eighteen respondents, I regarded the most favored answer (e.g., "R") as *"electing"* that verdict if ten or more chose "R."

At Oxford, only 7 items were thus "elected," the other 13 showing no overall majority. Even so, the "majorities" were usually slender: 6 of the 7 "elected" items received "votes" of only from 10 to 12 out of a possible maximum of 18. At Durham, with 10 dons participating, 8 items were elected. But when the results for Oxford and Durham were pooled, only 4 items showed majorities. When the Toronto results (with over 100 undergraduates participating) were combined in the same way, still less agreement resulted. Only items 1 and 14 evoked substantial agreement from the entire group of participants ("rational" for items 1 and 14).

It might be objected that the lack of agreement in application revealed by my admittedly somewhat amateurish survey of usage resulted from the controversial nature of some of the examples used rather than from variations in the meanings attached to the rationality labels. I feel the force of this criticism, though I do not accept it. I would be much interested in the results of better investigations by some of my readers. But I am rather confident that further experiments will confirm my present conviction that 'rational' and 'irrational' are now used by laymen and professionals with striking lack of consensus.

A Linguistic Approach

I would not wish to leave the impression that I consider further investigation into rationality a hopeless task, in view of the extreme variations in available answers to the "fundamental question." On the contrary, I wish to recommend what might be called a "linguistic approach," having at least the advantage of relative novelty.

My proposal is to start, as none of the scholars to whom I have referred seem to think worthwhile, with an examination of how the *word* 'rational' and its cognates are actually used by ordinary persons, uncommitted to any theories about "the nature of rationality."

I hope it unnecessary to defend myself against the common and scornful objections of philosophers who use "Ordinary Language Philosophy" as a term of abuse. I do not wish to be a lexicographer and am rather interested in what the word 'rational' and its cognates *mean* (to use a simplistic and possibly misleading formula), i.e., in the notion or *concept* of rationality.

In so doing, I shall be agreeing with Peter Geach, in his Mental Acts.[13] But I shall not follow him in taking "having a concept" in a "subjective sense"—as "standing for a mental capacity belonging to a particular person" (p. 13), wishing rather to use 'concept' as we do when we say that two persons "have the *same* concept" (cf. Frege's *Begriff*). I am interested in the standard uses of the word in question, not in individual and possibly idiosyncratic deviations from such uses. This is an empirical program, normally requiring no fieldwork, since as competent users of English we can rely on "what we would say" and in which circumstances.

One of the many important lessons that linguists have learned from Ferdinand de Saussure has been to think of a language as a structured system—"an organized totality . . . in which the various elements are interdependent and derive their significance from the system as a whole."[14] A special case of this is that words "belonging to the same sphere" signify partly by way of opposition or contrast (so that 'red', for instance, implies not blue, green, and so on). Hence there arises the important but still somewhat neglected notion of a *semantic field:* "closely-knit sectors of the vocabulary, in which a particular sphere is divided up, classified and organized in such a way that each element helps to delimit its neighbors and is delimited by them" (according to Jost Trier, as reported in Ullmann, p. 245).

In the present context, we should need to use the related notion of a *conceptual field*, in which words belonging to "the same

13. Peter Geach, *Mental Acts* (London, 1967).
14. S. Ullmann, *The Principles of Semantics* (New York, 1957), p. 8.

sphere" can be linked not only by opposition, but also by subordination and superordination and other syntactic, semantic, and pragmatic relations.

Application to the Case of Rationality

In trying to delineate the conceptual field to which 'rational' and its cognates belong, we would be faced with a series of subtasks, such as the following:

First: which other concepts are logically and conceptually linked with rationality? The list should probably include, in addition of course to 'rational' and 'irrational', also 'reason', 'choice', 'action', 'decision', 'belief', 'attitude', 'feeling', 'risk', 'uncertainty', 'probability', 'worth', 'value' (and such modal notions as) 'shall', 'should', 'must,' and so on. (I am aiming here only at illustrations, not at completeness, if that idea even makes sense.) Even this partial list is formidable, already recalling something of the richness and complexity of the conceptual field to which our key words belong. We should also wish to explore the effects of metonymy, i.e., the admissible fillers for the context, 'rational such-and-such'.

An important part of the task of delineating the relevant conceptual field would be to consider the relation of 'rational' to such seminormative words as 'intelligent', 'sensible', 'thoughtful', 'well-considered', 'praiseworthy', and so on, and a corresponding list of terms and phrases of dispraise (e.g., 'hasty', 'biased', 'prejudiced', and many more).

Nor should we neglect such broader questions as "what roles do uses of 'rational', 'rationality', and their semantic allies and enemies play?" We need to understand the roles that the targeted words play in our language, thought, and actions and to consider what losses, if any, would result from banishing the examined concepts from our language and thought.

It would be foolish to predict the outcomes of such a program of research, here only incompletely sketched. But I shall venture to guess at the kinds of results to be expected.

*Rationality*

## How to Be Rational: The Case of the Chess Player[15]

I propose now to consider some features of what may be the best available extended example of practical rationality—the familiar and instructive one of a good chess player's behavior. For surely what good chess players do is as close to any ideal of attainable if imperfect rationality that we can reasonably entertain: compared with decisions made in the course of a chess match, the decisions made in private life, the marketplace, or a law court are bound to appear as necessarily fumbling and unsatisfactory.

The relative determinateness of the chess player's task of playing rationally by finding the "best move" arises, clearly, from the arbitrary and precise constraints imposed by the "rules of play," that generate sequences of "legal moves," normally too complex to permit exhaustive analysis. It is easy, however, to prove the surprising result that there must always be a "best" way to play, even though it is beyond human power to know what the optimal strategy is.[16] Thus the invariable outcome of any chess game with "best moves" on both sides must follow from the rules: a faultless encounter must always end in a win for White, a win for Black, or a draw—whichever of these is always the right answer.

But to know that this theoretical "solution" exists is of no help to an actual player, faced with a bewildering multiplicity of legal moves, beyond the powers of even a chess genius like Bobby Fischer to analyze exhaustively. If we assume no more than 10 reasonable possibilities for each move (i.e., roughly 3 moves to be considered by White, each of them leading to 3 reasonable replies), the number of possible games lasting 40 moves will be of

---

15. This section is excerpted from my paper "Some Remarks about Rationality," *Philosophic Exchange* 2 (1977).
16. Let a "strategy" for White (in game-theoretical style) denote a complete policy for playing the game, taking into account all possible replies by Black at every juncture. If there exists an optimal strategy for White (leading invariably to a win or a draw), he commits himself to that strategy and plays accordingly. If not, then for every first move by White, Black can adopt a strategy that defeats him. Thus with "best play" on both sides, there must be a single predetermined result (win for one player or a draw), the same in each case. For another indirect argument, see Morton D. Davis, *Game Theory* (New York, 1970), pp. 16–18.

*Ambiguities of Rationality*

the order of $10^{40}$ (one followed by 40 zeroes). It has been estimated that a billion machines examining a billion such games each second and in constant operation since the solar system came into existence would by now have achieved only one ten-millionth part of the task of scrutiny.[17] This mechanical mode of evaluation is clearly too preposterously difficult to be worth considering.

In the light of such considerations, one might reasonably conclude that chess is too difficult a game to be played rationally. Yet vast numbers of human beings, of moderate intellectual capacity, do manage to play the game with steady and deserved success. How, then, does a skillful player manage to perform this seemingly impossible task?

In answering the question, we can rely upon introspective evidence or, better still, upon the instructive "protocols" assembled and analyzed in Adriaan D. de Groot's pioneering book.[18] I have already said that a reasonably good player does not consider all the legal moves available to him and does not engage in extended sequential calculations of consequences except in especially "critical" junctures. Such essential simplification of the problematic situation requires what may be called a patterned or Gestalt-like perception of a given position: unless one is a mere beginner who "can't begin to imagine what should be done," one sees the relatively few "candidate-moves"[19] as salient possibilities against a highly structured background. The skilled player does not perceive a mere aggregate of squares occupied by pieces, but rather features describable in the distinctive (partly qualitative, partly quantitative) language of chess strategy and tactics: "a weak King," a "strong center," "batteries of pieces,"

---

17. Based on a discussion in C. H. O'D. Alexander, *A Book of Chess* (New York, 1973), p. 23.

18. Adriaan D. de Groot, *Thought and Choice in Chess* (The Hague, 1965). The author persuaded a number of chess players, including masters, of varying degrees of skill, to "think aloud" while examining a number of selected situations and chess positions. The records thus obtained were the "protocols" (supplemented by subsequent discussion with their producers).

19. I take this expression from a later book by a grandmaster, which interestingly supplements de Groot: Alexander Kotov, *Think Like a Grandmaster* (London, 1971).

"open files," and so on. Such a patterned grasp of the situation, reinforced by memories of parallel situations and their outcomes, distinguishes a few moves as alone worth consideration and rejects others as being, at least initially, unworthy of consideration.

Of course, a skillful player will proceed to calculate the likely consequences of each of the limited number of "candidate-moves" that are initially judged to be worth taking seriously. But in an actual game (by contrast with the protracted sessions in which masters aim at exhaustive analysis of "adjourned games") such analysis of anticipated consequences is necessarily truncated and incomplete. It is worth making the further point, familiar to any good player, that such analysis may well modify or radically transform one's view of the given position: attempts to solve the perceived problem are apt to change one's conception of the nature of the problem. The process of rational choice is dynamic—to use a word that has perhaps been overworked in the literature.

The dynamic process of finding a rational solution to a problem of decision in playing chess does not and cannot occur in an intellectual vacuum: a chess player with a tabula rasa, wiped clean of all preconceptions and preformed convictions, would almost certainly succumb in short order to a "Fool's Mate" or some comparably ignominious fiasco. Any moderately instructed player is strongly guided by memories of his own previous successes and failures and, still more importantly, by the sifted experience of whole generations of masters. The accessible tradition supplies defeasible general maxims, standardized routines for accomplishing particular subtasks, detailed models for the initial deployment of pieces (the "opening"), and much else. Such deliverances of a rich tradition can function as premises of the requisite "practical reasoning" and usually need not be questioned, but any of them *can* be questioned and perhaps rejected in special cases. (Here, we are far from the unquestioned premises of Russell's model.)

Such reliance upon traditional deliverances, used in a not uncritical situation, surely supplies the good chess player with "good reasons," however inconclusive, for his choice: it would be eminently unreasonable to ignore the available experience of past players, however fallible and defeasible the lessons to be drawn from them may be.

The necessary reliance in such concrete exemplifications of practical reasoning on what might be called "indubita"—premises stronger than mere presuppositions of working assumptions—seems to be quite characteristic and typical of available instances of extended rational choice.[20]

Envoi

Any reader who might expect me to end with a concise answer to the "fundamental question" will have to be disappointed. I believe it is fair to say that in philosophical discussions of rationality, there is a sense in which we do *not* "know what we are talking about" and can never do so, if what is demanded is a concise definition. To provide one would be as difficult and as pointless as demanding an initial or terminal definition of playing chess well (or understanding poetry, or behaving morally, or leading the good life). But there is a less stringent sense in which we do initially understand, however sketchily, what we mean by playing chess well—and the same applies, mutatis mutandis, to the still more complex notion of rationality, whether in private or in public contexts. I would be sorry to be taken as opposing further analytic investigation of the role of rationality in appropriate contexts. On the contrary, I believe that much remains to be learned about this important if elusive notion.

Appendix: Rationality and Irrationality:
A Questionnaire

The purpose of this questionnaire is to get some empirical evidence about how people apply the words 'rational' and 'irra-

20. Current efforts to simulate chess-playing skill in computer programs sensibly ignore cost-benefit analysis, trying instead to incorporate the requisite knowledge of tactics and strategy to which I have alluded. Such programs try, although with only moderate success so far, to take account of the "patterned perception" and reliance upon maxims of play that I have emphasized.

Rationality

tional'. Each of the following 20 items identifies something *you* might do. In each case, you are asked to say whether you consider doing so would be rational or irrational. Please answer by writing a capital letter to the left of the item number, according to the following code: R = 'rational'; I = 'irrational'; N = 'neither'; C = 'can't answer'; U = 'undecided how to answer'.

Please answer all the questions. Comments, which will be welcome, may be written on the back of the sheet. Especially helpful would be (i) explanations of answers; (ii) comments on choice and formulation of items; (iii) suggestions for improving the questionnaire.

_____ 1. To presume that a stranger of whom you have asked directions is answering truthfully.
_____ 2. To envy somebody else for his/her good looks.
_____ 3. To be satisfied with a good outcome of a task when you might expect a better result at little cost.
_____ 4. To pay $30 for a one-in-a-thousand chance of winning $50,000.
_____ 5. To think that an argument with false premises will have a false conclusion.
_____ 6. To let somebody die in a fire rather than risk burning your hands in trying to save him.
_____ 7. To resent injury done to you.
_____ 8. To enjoy music played as loudly as possible.
_____ 9. To think that life exists elsewhere in the universe.
_____ 10. After an ordinary coin has been tossed and has come down heads 5 times in succession, to expect it to do the same the next time.
_____ 11. To be afraid of spiders.
_____ 12. To prefer X to Y, Y to Z, and Z to X.
_____ 13. To think that somebody else is happier than you.
_____ 14. To bet on a horse winning and also, at the same odds, on its losing.
_____ 15. To like someone for no assignable reason.
_____ 16. To refuse to argue about whether friendship is a good thing in itself (regardless of its contributions to other things).

____ 17. To refuse to bet on a certainty.
____ 18. To regret a past action that cannot be undone.
____ 19. To try to construct a perpetual motion machine.
____ 20. To answer this questionnaire.

# 6

## The "Prisoner's Dilemma" and the Limits Of Rationality

*Hell is paved with good calculations.*

Anon.

### The Problem Introduced

The so-called Prisoner's Dilemma[1] is usually introduced by some such story as the following:

> Two men suspected of committing a crime together are arrested and placed in separate cells by the police. Each suspect may either confess or remain silent, and each one knows the possible consequences of his action. They are: (1) if one suspect confesses and his partner does not, the one who confessed turns state's evidence and goes free and the other one goes to jail for twenty years. (2) If both suspects confess, they both go to jail for five years. (3) If both suspects remain silent, they both go to jail for a year for carrying concealed weapons—a lesser charge. We will suppose that there is no

Reprinted, by permission, from *International Studies in Philosophy* 10 (1978), pp. 7–22.

1. The Dilemma was originally presented by Professor Albert W. Tucker of the Princeton University Department of Mathematics, in a talk given to graduate students of psychology at Stanford University in the spring of 1950. The game matrix had been drawn to Tucker's attention a little earlier by M. Dresher and M. M. Flood at the Rand Corporation but was "dressed up" by Tucker with a story to "catch psychological interest." The payoffs in the original version were 1, 0 −1, and −2 units (personal communication from Professor Tucker).

## The "Prisoner's Dilemma"

'honor among thieves' and each suspect's sole concern is his own self-interest. Under these conditions, what should the criminals do?

The paradox lies in this. Two naive prisoners, too ignorant to follow this compelling argument [for confessing] are both silent and go to prison for only a year. Two sophisticated prisoners, primed with the very best game-theory advice, confess and are given five years in prison in which to contemplate their cleverness.[2]

The story seems to show that irrationality sometimes pays better than rationality. Fools who rush in, happily ignorant of game theory, may do better than angels who calculate. But is that cause for alarm? The possibility, vividly illustrated by the fable, that rational decision can be detrimental to the satisfaction of self-interest and the achievement of mutual good, is too disturbing to be accepted without careful examination.

Predicaments of criminal conspirators would have little interest for the law-abiding, but for the wide incidence of what might be called, in Kantian style, an antinomy of rational choice. It is disconcerting that an intelligent prisoner must be thwarted by knowing in advance that his best calculations, echoed by those of his equally rational confederate, will necessarily result in harm to both, while a mutually beneficial outcome was there all the time for the taking, as it were.

If this is a predicament in which stupidity succeeds better than intelligent rationality, would it not be more intelligent after all to pretend to be stupid and act accordingly? No: for the other "player" cannot be counted upon to do likewise, if he is intelligent enough to see the advantage of profiting from the other's "stupidity", whether real or pretended. In this kind of situation, it will pay to behave "stupidly" only if one can count on the other doing likewise. Only two genuinely naive prisoners will prosper.

Especially disconcerting to those who have only modest expectations of benefit from altruistic or socially cooperative action is the apparent inexorability with which, in Prisoner's Dilemma situations, rational pursuit of self-interest generates an outcome detrimental to sheer self-interest. That selfishness can be its own nemesis may have been an edifying commonplace for old-style

2. Morton Davis, *Game Theory* (New York, 1970), pp. 93, 94.

moralists, but it is an uncomfortable admonition when there is no better resource than to pursue self-interest.

Generality of the Paradox

Antinomies of rational choice are endemic. In such varied contexts as voter apathy, destruction of natural resources by competitive exploitation and, most disturbingly, in armament races, short-term rational calculation proves to be the enemy of lasting good.[3] Allegedly rational abstention from voting, or participation in producing any other public good, damages and ultimately destroys the social arrangements upon which "free riding" is parasitic; reckless extraction of raw materials ultimately destroys profit as well as social benefit; cancerous proliferation of weapons, dictated by supposedly rational mistrust of other nations, yields no "equilibrium" except the apocalyptic one of mutual destruction.

In such cases, are we to conclude that hardheaded self-interest is necessarily self-defeating? And are there any alternatives to the pursuit of self-interest? Before concluding that rational decision makers have no other options and must sometimes be the victims of their commitment to self-interested rationality, it would be well to explore thoroughly the latent resources of an imaginative rationality, unconstrained by the supposedly inescapable conditions of a given "game." I hope to show, in the following discussion, that the lessons to be drawn from the Dilemma are somewhat less discouraging than they have sometimes been taken to be.

The Purpose of This Discussion

The "Theory of Games," as initiated in 1944 by Von Neumann and Morgenstern's treatise, concerns strategical situations in

3. Game theory analogies have even been used suggestively in discussions of natural selection between individuals and groups. See, for instance, J. M. Smith's interesting essay "Game Theory and the Evolution of Fighting," in his *On Evolution* (Edinburgh, 1970).

which individual outcomes, or payoffs, result from the interdependent choices of several agents trying to anticipate and extract advantage from one another's choices.

According to a widely accepted but erroneous methodological dogma, any theoretical discussion of the "strategical" aspects of human action that concern game theory (or, for that matter, any theoretical discussion in the social sciences) must necessarily aim at being either descriptive or prescriptive. The dogma alleges that unless game-theoretical conclusions are approximately true empirical generalizations about how human decision makers behave, those conclusions must be regarded simply as exhortations addressed to would-be rational strategists.[4] (For instance: if there is a mixed-strategy "solution" to a two-person zero sum game, a rational player should resort to a probability mixture of "pure strategies" in the indicated proportions). But, considered as empirical assertions, game-theoretical conclusions are typically false; and considered as advice, they provoke serious objection. I reject this Hobson's Choice: I shall not predict how entrapped prisoners *will* behave and shall refrain from presumptuous admonitions as to what they *ought* to do.

There is, however, another task worth pursuing under the rubric of game theory: that of exploring the *logical and mathematical implications* of such basic concepts as preference, utility, and rationality which all decision makers, more or less explicitly and consistently, use. With such a commitment—which need not interfere with any empirical or prescriptive interest—the procedures of game theory, and of the particular discussion here

---

4. A recent writer, in connection with his discussion of the Prisoner's Dilemma, more cautiously distinguishes between "discourse about the empirical world (positive discourse), discourse about what is logically necessary (roughly the same as pure mathematics), and ethical or aesthetic discourse (discourse which makes value judgments)": Nigel Howard, *Paradoxes of Rationality* (Cambridge, Mass., 1971), p. 48. He traces the source of the dilemma to our wishing "that 'rational behavior' . . . be simultaneously the way people *do* behave, the way that logically they *must* behave, and finally the way they *should* behave" (p. 49). Howard, mistakenly in my judgment, dismisses the "logical" mode of discourse as "a sterile procedure that inevitably means defining the problem by defining our terms so that, not only the behavior in question, but any behavior whatever would be consistent with our theory" (ibid.).

initiated, will be *explicative*[5] and *analytical:* explicative, because the goal is heightened understanding of the concepts under investigations; analytical, because the yield will consist, at least in part, of "analytically true" or "necessary" propositions. Such an inquiry might be called *conceptual analysis*. The goal will be greater clarity, not empirical prediction or practical advice. Yet clarity or intellectual grasp of the kind envisaged will also have immediate consequences for the predictive and prescriptive preoccupations of game theory: the explicative propositions delivered by the conceptual inquiry will readily generate empirical, explanatory, and prescriptive assertions for those who want them. To the extent that decision makers actually try to behave rationally, explicative conclusions concerning the conceptual structure of rationality will facilitate relatively precise empirical assertions concerning observable actions. Again, if decision makers are trying to be rational, the explicative conclusions can provide *explanations* of their actions from the agents' own standpoint and if one believes that agents *should* behave rationally (e.g., by seeking to maximize their preferences, wherever possible), corresponding prescriptions will at once be at hand. But an explicative analyst is well-advised to hold such empirical or prescriptive corollaries in reserve, attending mainly to the sufficiently demanding task of furthering conceptual clarity.

As a paradigmatic instance of explicative analysis one might invoke mathematical geometry. It would be absurd to exhort material bodies to conform to geometrical theorems; but we need not therefore conceive of geometry as a *description* of the spatial relations between idealized material bodies. Geometry can, at least as plausibly, be viewed as a conceptual system exhibiting, in often surprising ways, the logical consequences of the features of the basic spatial concepts that are captured by the axioms. That is why geometrical propositions are properly recognized to be a priori and why the methods of geometrical analysis and proof are wholly free of empirical admixture. *Mutatis mutandis*, the same can be said of the methods and conclusions of conceptually ori-

---

5. The allusion to Carnap's "explication" is deliberate. See his excellent discussion of this topic in *Logical Foundations of Probability* (Chicago, 1950), pp. 3ff.

ented game theory, viewed as a kind of geometry of strategic action. There, too, we can seek to elaborate the logical consequences of certain axioms, regarded as partial specifications of the concepts in question—without prior commitment to empirical adequacy.[6]

More specifically, I shall be concerned with the following questions: First, what would *count* as rational action in the kind of recalcitrant case illustrated by the Prisoner's Dilemma? The method to be employed calls for the logical and mathematical elaboration of the implications of some provisionally adopted conception of rationality.

Although the prime object is to clarify *our own* conceptions of rationality by applying them to hard cases, we are not bound to rest satisfied with any limitations of rationality that may be revealed. Unsatisfactory or unwelcome implications can reasonably be regarded as indicating defects in the received conception of rationality and so as spurs to the construction of improved conceptions. So a second question will be: In the light of the implications for rationality uncovered by the "hard cases," can our working conceptions of rationality be regarded as satisfactory? And if not, how are they to be improved or replaced? Is the fault in our ideals of rationality? Or does the nature of things set absolute limits to their applications?

General Analysis of Prisoner's Dilemma Situations

In order to avoid distraction by decorative but irrelevant details of the Prisoner's Dilemma fiction, I shall henceforth refer to exemplifications of the antinomy of rational choice as *entrapment situations:* E-situations for short. The simplest E-situation will, accordingly, be one in which two individual or "corporate" persons—say "Row" and "Column"—must make independent one-shot choices, whose outcomes are shown in the following familiar matrix.

---

6. I have eschewed the overworked term "model." Some writers would prefer to characterize the approach I am advocating as one of constructing models, while suspending considerations of empirical applicability.

*Rationality*

*Table 1.* Generalized structure of two-person E-situations

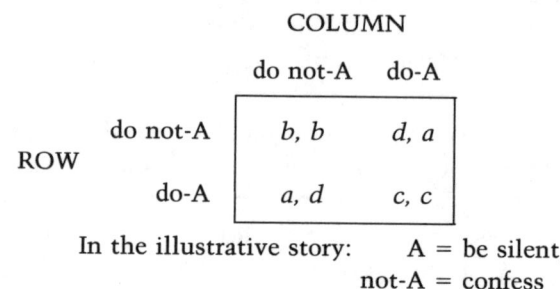

In the illustrative story:   A = be silent;
                              not-A = confess

It is assumed that each contestant prefers $d$ to $c$, $c$ to $b$, and $b$ to $a$ ($d > c > b > a$). Also, the players are supposed to have no communication, choosing what to do in ignorance of each other's choices. The first line of the table shows that if Row and Column do not-A, each gets a payoff of $b$; while if Row does not-A and Column does not, the first gets a payoff of $d$, but the second a payoff of $a$; and similarly for the other two entries in the table. We can ignore the troublesome problems raised by specification of the contestants' utilities and the interpersonal comparability of such utilities, since the simpler and more abstract scheme that follows will suffice for our present purpose.

It is worth noticing, however, that the relative values of the magnitudes $a$, $b$, $c$, $d$ can make a significant difference in practice to the choice of a defensible strategy—especially so if the situation or game is iterated (allowed to recur a number of times). For instance, if the risk $b-a$, is small, it will be more reasonable—at least in reiterated plays—sometimes to do A (at the risk of receiving no more than $a$) in the hope that the other will cooperate in producing the mutually advantageous outcome $c$, $c$. Should the temptation, $d-b$, be considerable (and so the reward for a double-cross correspondingly high), such a cooperative gambit will be correspondingly riskier.[7]

Let us, however, ignore these interesting complications for the

---

7. Here I am indebted to Phillip Bonacich's stimulating paper "Putting the Dilemma Back into Prisoner's Dilemma," *Journal of Conflict Resolution* 15 (1970), pp. 379–87.

present and now tabulate only the relative preferences of the contestants:

*Table 2.* Ordinal structure of two-person E-situations

|  |  | COLUMN | |
|---|---|---|---|
|  |  | do not-A | do-A |
| ROW | do not-A | 2, 2 | 4, 1 |
|  | do-A | 1, 4 | 3, 3 |

The numbers now simply indicate *the orders of preference* of the outcomes for each contestant (with 4 the highest). All questions about utilities or their comparisons are bypassed. It will sometimes be convenient to reproduce such a matrix in the following abbreviated from: (2,2 / 4,1 / 1,4 / 3,3).

Table 2 will quickly show why Row and Column, acting out of rational self-interest, must both do not-A and so produce the outcome 2,2—which is the third best result for each. For Row sees at once that the first line "dominates the second," as game theorists say: he will do better by choosing to do not-A rather than A, *no matter what Column does:* if Column does not-A, Row ends with 2 rather than 1; and if Column does A, Row ends with 4 rather than 3. So Row has a sure thing in doing not-A, with nothing to lose, comparatively speaking, no matter what happens. He will therefore do not-A.

Given the symmetry of the E-situation, and the corresponding symmetry of the matrix in Table 2, Column has an exactly parallel argument. For him, the first column dominates the second: he, too, will do better by choosing not-A rather than A, no matter what Row does: if Row does not-A, Column gets 2 rather than 1 and if Row does A, Column gets 4 rather than 3. So, like Row, he does not-A—and both end at 2,2—while, of course, each would prefer 3,3.

There are a number of ways of elaborating the dominant features of the preferred strategies and thereby rendering prominent the force of these parallel arguments and the stability of the resulting joint choice.

*Rationality*

(1) No additional information about the way in which the other contestant will in fact decide can impugn the rationality of choosing not-A: if Column is in fact foolish enough to do A, it will still have paid Row to do not-A, since he then gets 4 rather than 2. Thus it might be said that Row's decision to do not-A is objectively as well as subjectively rational, for although he acts in partial ignorance, not knowing what Column will do, that lack of knowledge makes no difference: an omniscient predictor would still choose not-A.

(2) Any unilateral deviation from the rationally preferred action (doing not-A) is bound to be punished: in the language of game theorists, the outcome 2,2 is an "equilibrium point."

It has sometimes been suggested that there is a way out of this inexorable reasoning to an unappetizing conclusion (for after all, Row and Column would both prefer 3,3—if only it could be reached) if the postulated conditions of independent choice are relaxed to permit consultation. Why should the two contestants not agree in advance to choose A, to their mutual benefit? The standard and persuasive answer is that it will then pay each of them to violate such an agreement: indeed, if either has reason to think that the other will choose A (perhaps because he is the sort of person who honors agreements), there will be all the more reason to choose not-A, with the expectation of even higher profit (4 rather than 2). To be sure, it is sometimes possible to enter into binding agreements, i.e., to arrange that the cost of violation is greater than the advantage reaped: if money is at stake, a suitable sum can be placed in escrow, as a guarantee against violation; if liberty is in question, criminals can ensure fidelity by having an "enforcer" to kill the traitor. But such devices, whatever their practical importance, have usually been said (and with justice) to change the original dilemma. If double-crossing is made less attractive than reaching the outcome in the bottom right-hand cell, we have the new matrix: (3,3 / 1,2 / 2,1 / 4,4). Here the double-cross action—not-A chosen against A—has been made the least preferred outcome for each: there is no longer a dominating strategy; but minimax considerations lead both contestants to the outcome 4,4 in the bottom right-hand corner, i.e., the one that both now regard as the best. I shall assume, for the time being, that this objection is well-founded and that the dilemma or paradox is not plausibly to be circumvented by changing the rules—although I shall eventually try to argue that in some sense it may be rational to transform the game rather than wring one's hands at its unwelcome outcomes.

E-Situations with More than Two Participants:
The Inaccessibility of Common Goods

A natural extension of the notion of an E-situation is to cases involving more than two persons, each of whose strategical choices vis-à-vis the others (taken singly or collectively) has the "paradoxical" structure exemplified in the ordinal version of the Prisoner's Dilemma. Among the most interesting and practically important examples of such "multiple E-situations," as they might be called, are (a) provision of a common good that requires individual contributions, and (b) voting in large elections. Let us consider these in turn.

(a) *Collective action for a common good.* Suppose ten householders are proposing to construct a sidewalk, which will be a common good because it will benefit each member of the group. Suppose the total cost of the work is 10 units and its value to each householder is $20/10 = 2$ units, so that each stands to gain 2 units of benefit for an outlay of 1.[8] Any one person in the group has the option of sharing in the cost (= doing A) or refusing to do so (= doing not-A). If the free-rider refuses to join in, the others will then either construct the sidewalk without him or simply choose not to proceed. Then the matrix looks as follows:

Table 3. Simplified structure of free-rider versus the rest

|  |  | OTHERS | |
|---|---|---|---|
|  |  | do not proceed | proceed |
| FREE-RIDER | does not pay | 0,0 | 2,8 |
|  | pays | 0,0 | 1,9 |

8. The case is taken, with unimportant modifications, from Russell Hardin, "Collective Action as an Agreeable n-Prisoner's Dilemma," *Behavioral Science* 16 (1971), pp. 472–81.

Clearly the first row dominates the second, and it is therefore rational for the prospective free-rider to let the others carry the burden. If they proceed he will get his share of the common benefit at no cost to himself (2 units of gain instead of 1). The same verdict obviously also results from a more detailed analysis in which Free-rider considers the consequences of any number 0 to 9 of the others proceeding with the plan alone.

Table 3 also shows that the second column dominates the first, so that it would be *collectively* rational for the others to proceed without Free-rider—and to swallow their mortification at seeing him get away with a disproportionate and unfair share of the net benefit (2 units instead of 1, leaving only 8/9th unit net benefit for each of the others). However, it is to be presumed that each of the others will calculate his prospects vis-à-vis the others in the style of Table 3. Thus each will decide rationally to abstain and the end-product will be the situation 0,0 for everybody. The end-results are typical of E-situations: rational calculation puts each of the participants in an equilibrium position that is less desirable to each than the unattainable position in which each ends up with a positive net benefit.

(b) *The irrationality of voting*. Assume a large election that cannot be decided by a single vote. Suppose that a potential voter, Democrat, is considering whether to vote: and let the others be the remaining voters who would vote on the same side of the question. Then Democrat can argue as follows: "If we—those who vote on my side of the question—fail to win, my vote has achieved nothing and if we do win, then we would do so, even if I abstained. So in either case, I can spare myself the cost (in time and expended energy) of voting: I have nothing to gain in either case." But of course, if all the other members of Democrat's side perform the same calculation and stay at home, they will collectively lose their common good (the chance of having their preferred candidate elected—or, perhaps the certainty of doing so).[9] Complications aside, this is a pattern similar to that of the last case. Each potential voter is in a typical E-situation in which

9. This so-called paradox of voting has been much discussed. For a recent analysis, see, for instance, W. H. Riker and P. C. Ordeshook, *An Introduction to Positive Political Theory* (New York, 1973).

"rationality" dictates an action that is unsatisfactory for each and potentially disastrous for all.

What the Pundits Say

The responses of social scientists and philosophers who have reflected upon the structure of E-situations can be classified as follows: (1) cheerful or resigned acceptance; (2) invocation of some extrarational criterion of action.

(1) Some writers see nothing to deplore or regret in the prevalence of E-situations. Indeed, some of them refuse to see in these situations anything that needs to be called either a "dilemma" or a "paradox." Thus R. L. Cunningham writes: "There is nothing wrong about the rational choice for any prisoner, given the conditions of the game, though of course both prisoners might like to play some other sort of game"[10]—though he adds, later, that society might prefer that they remain entrapped. And again he thinks it "obvious that there are no better grounds for calling the Prisoner's Dilemma a paradox than there are for calling it a dilemma. And I fail to see that in a two-person non-zero-sum game, the 'rational' choice is somehow contraindicated or has less prescriptive power."[11] In other words, it may be uncomfortable to be trapped in an E-situation, but if one is trapped the correct thing to do is to choose the rational strategy—and not waste time on futile regrets at not being in some better situation. It is in this spirit that Luce and Raiffa say: "No, there appears to be no way around the dilemma. We do not believe there is anything irrational or perverse about the choice of [the dominant strategy] and we must admit that if we were actually in this position we would make these choices."[12]

(2) On the other hand, many writers find such "realistic" ac-

---

10. R. L. Cunningham, "Ethics and Game Theory: the Prisoner's Dilemma," *Papers on Non-Market Decision-Making* 2 (1967), pp. 11–26.
11. Ibid., p. 14.
12. R. Duncan Luce and Howard Raiffa, *Games and Decisions* (New York, 1957), p. 96.

quiescence in "rational" choice—even when it leads to predictable disaster "intuitively unacceptable."[13]

Some writers hold that "rational" strategic choices may flout morality. Thus, Anatol Rapoport, who has argued most eloquently for "a dialogue . . . between strategy and conscience," says: "In spite of occasional protestations on the part of strategists that their job is rational analysis, not value judgments, value judgments are unavoidably included in their analysis, because the end results of these analyses are policy recommendations."[14]

Virginia Held has urged that "it is *reasonable*, if not demanded by rationality itself, to do that which is in the interests of others when it is *no less* in the interests of ourselves" and that "if this adds to rationality some element of morality, this is . . . appropriate for the concept of the reasonable."[15]

Frederic Schick has suggested that we need to invoke a concept of "sociality," so defined that a person is "behaving socially if and only if he is choosing as he thinks some other person or group of people want him to choose, and choosing so because he thinks this *independently of any consideration of the consequences he foresees*."[16] According to Schick's conception of rationality, a

---

13. Anatol Rapoport and Albert M. Chammah, *Prisoner's Dilemma* (Ann Arbor, Mich., 1965), p. 23.
14. Anatol Rapoport, *Strategy and Conscience* (New York, 1964), pp. 192, 191.
15. Virginia Held, "Rationality and Social Cooperation," in *Problems of Choice and Decision: Proceedings of a Colloquium Held in Aspen, Colorado, June 24–July 6, 1974*, ed. Max Black (Ithaca, N.Y., 1975), pp. 258–93.
16. Frederic Schick, "Rationalist Social Analysis: Some Hard Cases," in ibid., pp. 196–234.

It might be objected that the proposed solution is unsatisfactory in requiring the first prisoner (say A) to make only a conditional commitment, while the other (B, say) is required to make a categorical and possibly more risky response. Thus if
$$p = \text{I (A) am innocent}$$
and
$$q = \text{He (B) is innocent,}$$
A is supposed to assert $p \equiv q$ (I am innocent if and only if he is innocent), with the hope of inducing B to assert $q$.

Let us then slightly complicate the proposed way out by having A assert instead:
$$r = p \equiv (p \equiv q)$$
in the hope of inducing the symmetrical reply
$$s = q \equiv (q \equiv p).$$

person is "acting rationally whenever he is acting, in the light of his beliefs, so as best to serve his interests, whatever his beliefs and his interests are." According to him, therefore, "rationality" excludes "sociality." Nevertheless, Schick finds an escape from the Prisoner's Dilemma, if the players will eschew rationality in favor of sociality: if the other victim is a close friend who will want me to cooperate for our mutual benefit, then I will do what he wants because I should do so—and without regard for any consequences. And if both of us act in this way, "irrationally" but admirably, both of us will in fact benefit. This is a case, then, where moral virtue yields an immediate reward.

It may be doubted whether such attempts to show that rationality is insufficient for the resolution of E-situations have much hope of successful application. If we could count on entrapped contestants suppressing rational self-interest in the service of broader moral interests or the common good, the "paradoxical" features of such situations would melt away. But the practical obnoxiousness of E-situations arises precisely from the fact that the parties at dispute cannot, as a general rule, be counted upon to be "reasonable" or "social"—cannot be counted upon to take the risks that necessarily attend any straying from the strategy of rational self-interest. It will therefore be worthwhile to consider further whether all the resources of such self-interested strategy have been sufficiently examined in the available analyses.

A Possible Way Out?

Let us revert to the original example of the Prisoner's Dilemma. We assumed lack of communication between the prisoners. But we noticed also that, according to the accepted analyses, such communication (with corresponding possibilities of agreements

---

It will be found on consideration that $r$ is (surprisingly) equivalent to $q$; while $s$ is similarly equivalent to $p$. Hence the joint assertion of $r$ and $s$ by the two prisoners is tantamount to silence or declarations of innocence by both. In this way out each prisoner, as it were, puts himself in the question of asserting the innocence of the other.

*Rationality*

between the contestants) would not provide an escape from the dilemma.

Let us, therefore, now suppose that such communication is permitted (as in many E-situations) and imagine Column to conceive the project of *unilaterally committing himself to cooperate* with Row, that is, to confess if he confesses and to be silent if he does. This conditional choice need not take the form of a promise to Row. Column, if permitted, might say to the District Attorney: "I did just as the other did—I participated in the crime if and only if he did." (For a real-life analogue to such conditional moves one might consider the practice of correspondence-chess players of sending their opponents alternative replies to possible moves: "If you play P-K4, I play N-KB3, and if not, I play PQ4." In such cases the player making the conditional move is *committed in advance*, and his opponent, knowing this, knows for certain the immediate consequences of the moves at his disposal.) Then, if Row knows that Column has committed himself unilaterally in this way, he will also know that the only possible outcomes of his own decisions are either 2,2 (if he himself confesses) or 3,3 (if he remains silent); rationality then dictates nonconfession—and the final outcome is 3,3.

One way of thinking about this suggestion is to regard Column's unilateral commitment as having changed the original game to the following one:

*Table 4.* Structure of modified Prisoner's Dilemma

|  |  | COLUMN | | | |
| --- | --- | --- | --- | --- | --- |
|  |  | —A/—A | —A/A | A/A | A/—A |
| ROW | do not-A | 2,2 | 2,2 | 4,1 | 4,1 |
|  | do A | 1,4 | 3,3 | 3,3 | 1,4 |

Here, an entry of the form X/Y for Column means that he adopts the strategy of playing X if Row chooses the first row, and Y if Row chooses the second. It will be noticed that in this new game Column has a dominating strategy in the first column (deciding to confess, no matter what Row does). So in choosing unilaterally the second column (the strategy of doing the same as Row) he is abandoning the possible advantage that would result from a double-cross on his part. Row, on the other hand, no longer has a dominant strategy. If he believes in Column's commitment, he would obviously do better to choose the second row. Otherwise, a "minimax" choice of taking the least risky decision will dictate choosing row one (where the worst that can happen is that he ends at 2,2—as in the original game). This means, however, that Column has *nothing to lose* by making his unilateral commitment: if he is believed, he will end at 3,3 as desired; if not, he will end at 2,2 and in no worse case than the expected outcome of the original game. *It is therefore rational for Column to make the commitment*—and Row's knowledge that it is rational, and that Column is running no risk in making it, should strengthen the chance that he will credit Column's declaration.

But perhaps we should reconsider. I said that Column, by introducing the new game, had abandoned the possible advantage in the original game of a double-cross on his part. It might, however, be also argued that Column has in fact relinquished *no* genuine advantage. For on the assumption that Row is rational, Column could forecast with certainty that the original game would end at 2,2; while, on the same assumption, he can forecast that the new game will end at either 2,2 or 3,3. (From Column's standpoint one might therefore say that the new game, by a natural extension of the term, *dominates* the first.) So, once again, Column has a sure thing in trying to get the new game played and in binding himself to make the cooperative move that he has announced. Such action is therefore altogether rational.

A possible objection to Column's enterprising attempt to change the rules of the game and so to escape from the deadlock of the original E-situation might concentrate upon the crucial issue of Column's credibility. It has been generally agreed by commentators on the original Dilemma that the deadlock could be broken by credible or, better still, binding agreements between the parties at issue. But if this has to be ruled out as unrealistic in the absence of sufficient confidence between the two sides, what is gained by putting the burden on one side (Row) to accept a unilateral declaration of intent? Well, joint agreements between mutually distrustful negotiators (who may not even be willing to discuss the issues) are notoriously hard to generate: on the action proposed, the difficulty of negotiations is eliminated and the remaining difficulty is narrowed to that of establishing the credibility of a single contestant. Furthermore, since it is to his interest to be believed, it is also to his interest to take (unilaterally) any steps that will irrevocably bind him to his conditional commitment. (And, once again, since the commitment becomes effective only on terms that he in any case desires, he has nothing at all to lose by such binding). The proposed change in the game has, accordingly, genuine advantages over acquiescing in the mutually disadvantageous terms of the original E-position.

The point can be generalized. Many situations can be described, and sometimes occur, in which a direct approach can only produce frustration. (An amusing example is the old story of the sheik who made his two heirs ride a race, with the stipulation that the fortune should go to the owner of the horse that came in last. The racers escaped from the dilemma by exchanging horses.) From the standpoint of a resourceful conception of rationality it is therefore rational to seek to change the rules of the game rather than to acquiesce in an imposed definition of the choices available.

## Application to the Case of Participation in a Common Good

In the illustration considered above (in conjunction with Table 3), those who wish to contribute equally to the common good might, in line with the "unilateral commitment" maneuver just discussed, commit themselves to join with all the others, provided *all* make the same commitment. As before, such a commitment can be made unilaterally without risk, since it will be implemented only on conditions that are desired by each individual participator. Consider now the situation in which nine of the ten householders, progressively strengthened in their unilateral resolves by the examples of the others, have already made the conditional commitment and only the would-be free-rider remains. He now has the choice between joining, in which case he gets a net benefit of 1 unit (sharing the costs equally with all the others) or staying out, in which case he gets nothing, like everybody else. So free-riding has been made unprofitable, and if the free-rider is rational, he will presumably join the others.

In order to obviate the possibility of the operation of such tiresome but genuine possibilities as dog-in-the-mangerism, the unilateral commitments might take the alternative form of conditional commitment to join in purchasing the common good if and only if, say, eight out of nine of the others agree to do likewise. This, to be sure, restores to the would-be free-rider the advantage of getting something for nothing by holding out to the last, but it retains the desirable feature of giving everybody who does not independently wish to profit at the expense of all a reason for making a conditional commitment. Thus it may be presumed that enough of the potential participants, by making a riskless conditional commitment, will in fact form a sufficiently large majority to render the joint project feasible—and without appeal to anything but self-interest.

Application to the Voting Case

Here the "unilateral" or, as it might also be called, "anticipatory" move can be approximately captured in the formula *voting in anticipation of sufficient others also voting*. Given that there is a common good to be obtained, but only if a sufficiently large number of voters actually go to the polling booth, it is rational for a individual voter first to make the conditional commitment (I will vote if enough of the others do) and then to assume that the antecedent of this conditional will in fact be satisfied (enough others will in fact vote). Here, as before, the possibility of a conditional unilateral commitment undercuts the force of the generalization objection ("Why should anybody else have any better reason to vote than you have?"). If I am not mistaken, it is rational for each interested voter to vote on the supposition that enough others will think the same. (I leave some of the obvious

*Rationality*

objections to this line of argument for discussion on another occasion.)

## Conclusion

If one has a choice, it is clearly rational to avoid getting into entrapment-situations of the type exemplified by the Prisoner's Dilemma. But if one is in fact entrapped, it is less than rational simply to accept the rules of the game as if they were inflexible natural constraints. For they are typically the outcomes of the perceptions of persons, that can in favorable circumstances be changed by appeals to shared interests, leaving in abeyance unpromising invocations of genuine moral concerns. The capacity of rational agents to transcend their own "mind-forged manacles" has been repeatedly demonstrated in mathematics, science, and technology. Such resourcefulness needs to be more generally recognized and built into our working conceptions of what counts as fully rational. I have tried to show, by making a positive suggestion for a way out of the Prisoner's Dilemma, that there is a reasonable prospect of success (at least in some cases) for such a transformation of the original conditions. So long as such a prospect exists, it is rational to try to achieve it. To expect that any such maneuver will in fact work is to expect too much. But then guaranteed success is not part of any acceptable conception of rational action.

# CHOICE THEORY

# 7

## *Making Intelligent Choices: How Useful Is Decision Theory?*

A long time ago, an enthusiastic scientist who taught me all the chemistry I have since forgotten, said something that has stuck in my memory: "Boys, remember that science can do anything for you, from choosing a horse to choosing a wife!" That seems in retrospect a curious choice of endpoints. It reminds me of an old saying, that England is heaven for horses and hell for women. Still, the ancient dream of using science to understand and even predict human choice—and above all to help us to make good choices—is now held by many experts to have been realized at last.

Bayesian Decision Theory, as it is usually called,[1] is the product of nearly four decades of intensive and ingenious work by economists, mathematicians, and philosophers. It has come to be widely used for policy evaluation in business and government. To cite one important example: in application to "cost-benefit analysis," it is the theoretical underpinning of President Reagan's remarkable Executive Order 12291 of 7 February 1981, which requires all "major" regulations by federal agencies to be supported by analysis of social costs and benefits, including those "that cannot be quantified," so that the chosen regulation involves "the least net cost to society."

---

Reprinted, in a slightly revised version and with added footnotes, by permission, from *The Bulletin of the American Academy of Arts and Sciences* 38, no. 2 (November 1984).

1. Some writers now prefer "subjective utility theory" as a title.

## Choice Theory

Bayesian theory has recently been acclaimed by Herbert Simon as "one of the impressive intellectual achievements of the first half of the twentieth century," and an "elegant machine for applying reason to problems of choice."[2] (From now on, I shall use "decision" and "choice" interchangeably, although they would need to be distinguished in a further discussion.)

I think in this connection of the ambition of the great Marquis de Condorcet, an eighteenth-century pioneer in mathematical sociology, to illuminate the moral and political sciences by "the torch of algebra" (*éclairer les sciences morales et politiques par le flambeau de l'algèbre*).

If Bayesian theory is sound, and we do now possess an "elegant machine" for generating rational choice, that should be of extraordinary interest. For the exercise of free and responsible choice must surely count as a supreme exercise of what makes us, *qua* rational animals, distinctively human. Choice is an exercise of freedom: Simone Weil said that "liberty, taking the word in its concrete sense, consists in the ability to choose."

I shall try to present and evaluate some of the basic features of contemporary Bayesian theory without dwelling on technical details. For lack of time, I shall talk only about choices made by a single person. This is indeed the right place to start, since *all* choices, whether they are made by proxy or result from the aggregated decisions of groups, must finally rest upon what individual persons decide to do: choosing, like blowing one's nose, is something one must do for oneself. Unless Bayesian theory successfully illuminates this simplest kind of choice, it cannot hope to do justice to the more complex and interestingly controversial cases of collective or interactive choices.

### How a Bayesian Chooses

Let us consider the oft-quoted description of a decision-making situation offered by James G. March and Herbert A. Simon.[3]

---

2. Herbert A. Simon, *Reason in Human Affairs* (Stanford, 1982), p. 3. Simon, however, has repeatedly stressed the limitations of Bayesian choice theory.

3. James G. March and Herbert A. Simon, *Organizations* (New York, 1958), p. 137.

## Making Intelligent Choices

1. When we first encounter the rational man of economics and statistical decision theory in the decision-making situation he already has laid out before him the whole set of alternatives from which he will choose his action. This set of alternatives is simply 'given'; the theory does not tell how it is obtained. . . .

[I shall call the decision-maker *Eligo* and the set of his or her "given" alternatives the *slate of options*.]

2. To each alternative is attached a set of consequences—the events that will ensue if that particular alternative is chosen. [In the special case to be considered, we] assume the decision-maker has complete and accurate knowledge of the consequences that will follow on each alternative. . . .

[I shall call this a case of *reliable* choice.]

3. At the outset, the decision-maker has a "preference-ordering" that ranks all sets of consequences from the most preferred to the least preferred.
4. The decision-maker selects the alternative leading to the most preferred set of consequences. . . .

[In case of a tie, Eligo will choose any *optimal* alternative, i.e., one to which no other alternative is preferred.]

So much for "reliable" choice with certain outcomes. When the situation is one of risky choice, in which Eligo relies only upon the estimated probabilities of the consequences, the Bayesian story is modified by introducing the interesting but problematic notion of "expected utility." Roughly speaking, this is measured by the desirability for Eligo of an uncertain consequence, multiplied by Eligo's confidence in its occurrence.

### Descriptive or Normative?

There is an important imprecision in March and Simon's Bayesian story. In referring to the decision maker's behavior, they use the indicative mood: he or she "has" a preference ordering, and "selects" a most preferred alternative. This has the flavor of a factual description, and the Bayesian story is indeed usually regarded as an empirical description. Yet if the Bayesian story is to be faithful to Eligo's actual train of thought, it will need to include normative questions—not merely "What *can* I do?" but "What should I do?"—and, of course, corresponding normative answers.

Another writer in the Bayesian tradition—Isaac Levi[4]—summarizes the guidance supplied by decision theory as follows:

> Bayes's Rule: An ideally situated decision-maker . . . ought rationally to pick that option (or one of those options) bearing maximum expected utility.

Applied to our special case, this becomes: a rational chooser should take the option he or she most prefers. If that sounds like a tautology, I must tell you that it really is a tautology.

The history of the evolution of Bayesian theory shows that its inventors have had a double purpose. The customary title of a "theory" of choice or decision suggests something analogous to any well-established scientific theory—say Newton's theory of gravitation—that is, an abstract and idealized account of how persons in Eligo's position do actually choose. Bayesian theory, when so regarded, should be empirically verifiable or falsifiable. However, there is now strong evidence that actual choosers often do not behave like good Bayesians.[5] This need not bother Bayesian theorists, who quickly pass from predicting how Eligo *will* behave to advice on how he or she *ought* to behave. Yet, given the ancient and well-entrenched view that "is" can never strictly imply "ought," such a transition must give us pause. Indeed, since decision makers act as free agents, who might choose otherwise—and indeed often do so in un-Bayesian ways—we are entitled to wonder what justification there is for insisting that they *ought* to conform to Bayesian precepts?

Let us consider the parallel question of how empirical scientific

---

4. Isaac Levi, *Gambling with Truth* (New York, 1974), p. 45.
5. D. Kahneman, P. Slovic, and A. Tverski, eds., *Judgment under Uncertainty: Heuristics and Bias* (New York, 1982). See also George Wright, *Behavioral Decision Theory* (Beverly Hills, Calif., 1984).

## Making Intelligent Choices

medicine can generate rules and precepts for healthy behavior. Imagine somebody suffering from diabetes who is advised by a doctor to take insulin. If the patient asks what would happen if he or she did not do so, the doctor can specify highly disagreeable consequences. In such a case the link between background scientific knowledge and useful advice is clear. The physician assumes that his patient accepts the encompassing objectives of seeking health and shunning avoidable sickness, and the related view that if one wants to avoid the misery of untreated diabetes one should take insulin. With this extra premise, the doctor's factual report of the consequences of rejecting insulin does yield normative conclusions.

A situation in which one is advised by a Bayesian counsellor how to choose is less perspicuous. There, an answer to a request for justification might be expected to run as follows: "If you don't follow the Bayesian precepts you will be behaving *irrationally.*" But what, one might retort, is so bad about that? Well, that will depend upon the interpretation ultimately given to the partially normative term "rational." Irrationality is not like pain. One would have to be a lunatic to ask what's so bad about pain. When it comes to irrationality, which is quite popular in advanced circles these days, it isn't clear what the penalty is for refusing to follow Bayesian advice.

In general, then, we see that scientific knowledge about the consequences of available human choices will yield what has, since Kant, been called hypothetical imperatives: available empirical knowledge, when coupled with some overarching objective yields directives and *constraints* on the advisable behavior of anybody who accepts that objective. If we then ask: What is the overarching objective of Bayesian choice, and what are the penalties for not behaving like a good Bayesian, a short answer will be: "To choose *rationally,* on pain of being inconsistent otherwise."

It may be helpful at this point to reflect on the dire consequences of violating the rules of arithmetic. If an anti-arithmetical skeptic asks, "Why shouldn't I say that three can sometimes equal one?" we can reply, "Try it and see what happens! If you still use the ordinary rules for adding, subtracting, multiplying, and dividing, you will soon find yourself having to say that one equals zero. And then all numbers will have to be viewed as having the same value, zero!"[6] So people who want to say that three sometimes equals one had better be careful, if by three they mean what the mathematician means. The tightly integrated arithmetical calculus becomes useless if one violates a single component. Revolutionaries who want to break the chains of correct arithmetic will quickly find themselves unable to count, and of course unable to use such measuring instruments as clocks, calendars, yardsticks, thermometers and the other paraphernalia of civilization—a policy that might suit St. Simeon Stylites or some other "pillar hermit," but not the members of even a very primitive culture.

### The Mathematical Model of Choice

The standard Bayesian model for risky individual choice is usually presented nowadays in the form of an axiom system, that is, as a set of axioms about unidentified entities later identified as options, and an unidentified relation later identified as preference. Although I shall anticipate the ultimately intended interpretations by referring to the mathematical entities in question as simple or complex *options*, connected by the relations of *preference* and, for convenience, *equivalence*, it is important to bear in mind that, in the uninterpreted model itself, the entities and relations can be any things or relations that satisfy all the axioms. When one speaks of *options* in the model, one might, for all that the axiom system specifies, think instead of masses or heavy bodies; instead of one option being *preferred* or being *equivalent* to another, one might instead interpret the model as dealing with masses heavier than or equal in weight to other bodies.

One set of conditions specified by the axioms arrange an individual's available options in a so-called *weak ordering*. For lack of

---

6. Thus: starting from 3 = 1, subtracting 1 from each side yields 2 = 0. Dividing both sides by two produces 1 = 0, from which it follows that any integer is a sum of zeros and hence zero.

time I shall have to skip many details. As a first approximation, we can make do with thinking of an option as analogous to a person's height, and the relations of preference and equivalence as analogous to the relations of greater and equal heights between persons.

Suppose that I wanted to take a group photograph of this distinguished audience. I might then ask you to arrange yourselves—presumably in the park outside—taking care that each of you stood behind anybody who was shorter. If the wavering ranks then "squared off," we would have a living illustration of a weak ordering. (I don't intend to try the demonstration or to cope with the predictably resulting shambles!)

A weak ordering of relative preference (or, for that matter, relative height, or cost, or temperature) doesn't yet determine the magnitudes of differences in degrees of preference (or, in our analogue, the corresponding differences in height). Further specification of the magnitudes of differences between options is achieved by introducing the notion of a *gamble*. Thus, in the language of the interpreted axiom system, we now think of the Bayesian chooser as disposing not only of simple options, say $o_1$ and $o_2$, but also of such complex or "mixed" options as that of receiving $o_1$ with probability $p$, and $o_2$ with the complementary probability $1-p$. By postulating in the axiom system that for any such gamble there must be available an equivalent simple option, we can generate measures of degrees of preference as well determined as the numbers on a thermometer. (To speak technically, we get an "interval ratio scale" in which only the ratios of numerical intervals remain constant—as when we shift from Fahrenheit to centigrade readings of temperature.)

When things are weakly ordered, they split up into *equivalence classes* (in our analogy, rows of persons equally tall). Call the ordering relation P. Then for any two things in different equivalence classes (persons unequal in height) we must have either xPy or yPx but not both (given two persons unequal in height just one of them must be taller than the other). Also, xPx never holds (one is never taller than oneself). Finally, and importantly for later discussion, the P-relation must be *transitive*, that is, xPy and yPz together always imply yPz (when one person is taller than another and the latter is taller than a third, then the first is always taller than the third). Failure of such transitivity results in a *cycle,* with xPy, yPz, and zPx all being true (three persons of unequal heights, such that the first is taller than the second, the second taller than the third, and the last taller than the first). Such a result is intuitively absurd when we interpret P as *taller than*. There is unfortunately too little time to pursue further details.

When the mathematical axioms are all satisfied, the measures attached to the options (measures of degree of relative preference) can be shown to be the values of a *utility-function*—unique, as mathematicians concisely say, "up to a positive monotonic transformation."

The kind of mathematical arrangement and measurement that I have sketched is enticing. If the relative strengths of a rational individual's preferences can indeed be determined—in principle—as accurately as height is, we can hope to replace the messy business of untutored intuition and imprecise everyday judgment by truly scientific measurement. The cardinal precept for the instructed decision maker then reduces to the simple injunction to maximize or optimize the value of his imputed utility function. (More precisely, the decision maker is to act *as if* working on a utility-function.)

Lacking in our analogy with height is the absence of a precise instrument like a yardstick—a "selectometer," as it were. But even this might be overcome by a suitable computer program. We can imagine a would-be rational and scientific decision maker first answering a series of questions to identify his or her actual preferences (and also, importantly for the case of risky choice, reporting whether the chooser would be satisfied to exchange an option with determinate outcome for a gamble on two options). Provided with enough such information, the computer could then calculate the utility function to whose maximization a rational chooser is supposed to be already quasi-committed. The machine will proceed to announce the correct decision: one might even be tempted to say that the computer will make the rational choice. An entrancing prospect.

## Some Notable Features of the Bayesian Story

Let us start with a general observation: Eligo's situation is depicted in the literature in a highly abstract fashion, being identified only as that of a person trying to choose rationally; nothing is said about how he or she obtains the set of "given" alternatives, nor is anything said about the reasons that induce a preference for one option rather than another. (It is sometimes said that Bayesian theory and advice are intended to be merely prudential or economic, deliberately ignoring moral or religious considerations, but this is an unwelcome and unnecessary restriction.)

Now for some more specific observations:

1. The situation, in the form here considered, is one of *solitary and self-oriented* choice: our ideal Bayesian is supposed to be on her or his own, like Robinson Crusoe, deciding merely on the basis of his or her own preferences and probability judgments.

This restriction does not, however, preclude taking account, in a social context, of the reactions and desires of others; but for our present restricted purpose, such other-regarding consequences are relevant only to the extent that they influence the soliloquizing decision maker's own thoughts, beliefs, desires, and actions. Thus, altruistic considerations are admissible on condition of generating corresponding individual desires in the decision maker. Consideration for others, while not excluded, must be transformed—distilled, as it were—into what the chooser momentarily wants to do.

I shall have to neglect strategical decisions, in situations where the possible outcomes will be partially determined by choices made by other rational agents, whose own rational calculations must be heeded.

2. The Bayesian story is intended to be static, rather than dynamic—or, in a current idiom, "synchronic" rather than "diachronic." It catches the decision maker in a single episode of decision, neither presupposing nor excluding concern for past precedent or future correction: nothing is said about the advisability of conforming to previous decisions or invoking general maxims. These, too, if relevant, must be distilled or alembicated into rea-

sons for immediate action. Thus, static Bayesian advice to a chessplayer concerns only *the next move*.

A defender of the Bayesian standpoint would, I suppose, reply that room is left for all these above-mentioned factors to play a role indirectly, by determining the instantaneously given pattern of the chooser's resultant preferences. Nothing in the story, it might be said, precludes concern for remote consequences, or conformity with long-term goals and ideals. The Bayesian theorist postulates only that, in a particular instant of decision, such considerations should be alembicated into determinate personal preferences. The theory's advocates wish to ignore at least temporarily the stage setting, paying no attention to such considerations as to what others might rationally and responsibly do in the agent's situation, whether the agent may not ultimately regret what now seems attractive, and such other complicating considerations. We are to look at the chooser and his or her problems as grappling in a given place and at a given time with a *single* decision.

3. It should be noticed that the story makes no provision for any criticism or "rectification" of the given pattern of preferences, nor does it provide in the case of "risky" choice for any criticism of assigned probability estimates, apart from a general insistence upon the joint compatibility of such assignments. The only constraint upon the parameters of utility and probability is intended to be overall *consistency*.

4. What qualifies a particular choice of the parameters as approvably rational is therefore envisaged as a sort of logical or quasi-logical harmony between all the parameters. Hence the tendency for Bayesian advocates to speak of a "logic of choice," as if only some kind of formal coherence, without regard to the substantive character of the desires and expectations determining the choice parameters, were relevant to the purpose in hand. One resourceful and ingenious theorist, in recommending to managers what he called "a modernized Bayes-Laplace theory [of rationality]," once said, "In a nutshell, rationality . . . means consistency."[7]

7. I. J. Good, "How Rational Should a Manager Be?" *Management Science* 8 (1962), p. 383.

I am reminded of an anecdote about somebody who was fairly reasonable in ordinary life except for one obsession—the firm conviction that he was dead. When friends' arguments failed to persuade him otherwise, one of them stuck a pin into him, causing him to bleed. "Well," he replied, "that just shows that dead men can bleed." There's consistency for you—but surely not rationality.

A conviction that the rules of rational choice are as unassailable as the rules of logic is no doubt partly responsible for the vogue of the Bayesian approach. But history has played an important part, although the family tree of the Bayesian model is curiously tangled.

The original appeal to utility can be traced back to Bentham and other philosophical utilitarians such as Mill and Sidgwick who refined and improved Bentham's advocacy of the greatest happiness principle. The notion of expected utility arose in connection with certain problems in games of chance—notably the so-called St. Petersburg paradox. Efforts of economists to develop a science of behavior have also played an important part, and especially their adherence to a neopositivistic and behavioristic methodology.

Applying the Model: Generating the Slate

The first step in applying the Bayesian model to a particular situation is to consider what I have called a "slate" of options, that is, a limited set of possible choices. Of course, we don't have to consider all possible choices. Anybody faced with a tiresome task will always have some evasive, eccentric, or even absurd ways of coping. Facing my income tax form, I can decide to go to bed until the urge to complete the tiresome job disappears, or simply tear the forms up. But an intelligent and responsible chooser will reject many of these available actions as too foolish or dangerous to be worth entertaining. A politician faced by reporters who accuse him of lying will need strong nerves to respond by sticking out his tongue.

How, then, is the restricted set of eligible choices generated? As

I have said, the Bayesian story treats this set, unhelpfully, as simply "given." Yet in many nontrivial decision problems, a prime difficulty is that of deciding how to define the problem by specifying the options. It will often be sensible not to crystallize the initial position prematurely, letting the set of alternatives worth considering emerge *pari passu* with the estimation of likely consequences. But let us suppose that it does pay in a given situation to start with a set of fixed and determinate options. How are they "given," and where do they come from?

Well, sometimes the alternatives seem to be supplied by others, and the decision maker does seem to have a slate that is literally given. When buying an airplane ticket, answering a true–false question in a questionnaire, or choosing a meal from a restaurant menu, it may look as if the set of options has been predetermined. But this is partly an illusion. For Eligo can always make the important meta-decision of deciding not to choose at all, if willing to take the consequences. Even if the dictated choice is offered in the comprehensive form of doing A, doing not-A, or "standing pat," the person concerned need not cooperate, need not play that particular game. Refusing to bid when playing bridge is not making a bid of "pass."

Even when the chooser does accept an imposed partitioning of alternatives and forgoes the option of the meta-choice, he or she need not accept the *terms* in which the alternatives are couched. Consider a jury member, constrained by judicial procedure to decide only whether a defendant is guilty or innocent, and forced to use those labels in framing a decision. While wrestling with the rights and wrongs of the case, one might wish to think in terms of compassion rather than justice. Or perhaps one sees the problem as basically one of maintaining one's own view in courageous opposition to the views of other jury members. How the situation is perceived will, in turn, determine the choice of relevant and salient pros and cons. A politician's decision whether to support proposed legislation will strongly depend on whether the nation's welfare or his own prospects of reelection seems the more important.

In general, then, what might look like an imposed choice still leaves some freedom to decide how to perceive one's situation.

This can be seen in a case least favorable to my contention, that of a chessplayer deciding how to move. Here, if anywhere, it might seem as if the move to be made must be viewed in the standard formulation of chess notation. Yet this is not so. The player may be wondering whether or not to make a move which will be canonically recorded as "Bishop takes Pawn." But his choice will be materially influenced by whether he conceives of that move as a "sacrifice" (a deliberate loss in strength for the sake of future advantage), or as a "psychological surprise" (a move objectively weak, intended to waste the opponent's precious time). And so on. Once having introduced psychological considerations, why ignore prudential and even moral ones? It may seem relevant that the opponent should not be humiliated by too sudden a defeat, or be medically jeopardized by suffering an induced heart attack. In general, decision problems in chess that are not stereotyped or routine may require attention to considerations ignored in the official rules of the game.

The point I have been making is familiar in contemporary philosophical literature under the rubric of "the same action under a variety of descriptions." I have been arguing here that the choice of a so-called intensional description is normally available to a chooser even in a conventionally well-defined situation, such as that of a chessplayer or a juryman. The upshot is that application of the Bayesian model presupposes some prior activity of what, with some reservations, might be called "preselection."

If such preselection had to be explicit and deliberate, there might be danger of a vicious infinite regress. But the preselection need not be deliberate and will usually be *implicitly* presupposed. Implicit or not, the Bayesian scheme cannot be made to fit such preselection and is not intended to do so. A decision to ignore morality in favor of prudence cannot plausibly be analyzed in terms of the allocation of differential utilities.

One strong objection to viewing what occurs during "preselection" in Bayesian style is the following. In the Bayesian story, the listed alternatives have to be mutually exclusive; but the considerations that arise in preselection typically overlap. Thus a physician who has diagnosed a malignant tumor might well wonder whether to give his patient the alarming news; in so wondering, he is raising psychological, moral, professional, and even legal issues. Such aspects, once brought to consciousness, typically interact; the patient's knowledge of his condition may have a beneficial or deleterious influence on the proposed treatment, and even the patient's ability to pay may be important. Such a "doctor's dilemma," to borrow Bernard Shaw's title, is not an "either-or." Praiseworthy resolution of the doctor's problem should be based upon joint attention to all aspects of the situation and may well require restructuring of the "slate" by the imaginative invention of new options. In such situations the Bayesian schema may be quite unhelpful. Would it really be sensible for a doctor to determine whether he prefers frankness to deception, and if so, how much, by following the standard Bayesian procedure of imagining what betting odds he would accept for a corresponding "probability mixture"? Well, perhaps.

A more radical argument against the applicability of Bayesian analysis of what I have been provisionally calling "preselection" is this. An *aspect-shift*, or a *change of perspective*, as one might call it (say from "This would be an enjoyable drink" to "I must be mad to break my promise to my children"), is not typically *chosen*, but is rather *perceived* when the new perspective thrusts itself into consciousness. (The process resembles what happens in shifting from seeing the rabbit rather than the duck in the famous duck-rabbit picture). The shift forces itself upon the attention, like an illumination. Once the hitherto unperceived aspect emerges one can, up to a point, choose to ignore it—or at least try to do so—but usually not to forget it. On the whole, then, "preselection" is a dangerous label for the process of coping with emergent aspect-shifts. I have harped upon "aspect shift" and "change in perspective" because they can induce significant changes of the chooser's pattern of preferences. To cite one particularly important case: a shift from "I might choose A" to "In doing so I will necessarily be *rejecting* B, C, and so on" (i.e., a kind of extended "opportunity cost") might alter my initial preference for A, especially in cases where one of the forgone options is *irretrievably* forgone. Even if I now do somewhat prefer A to B, I might still rather choose B if there will be a later chance of doing

A, but not B. (Here, of course, we shift from a static model to a dynamic one.)

Problems of Application

Let me suppose that some kind Bayesian theorist has presented me with a choice program conforming to the mathematical model, and that I have already plugged the program into my microcomputer. So when I go to my favorite liquor store to choose a new bottle of wine, all I need do (all!) is to feed the data reflecting my momentary preferences into the computer, which will then tell me what the "rational choice" should be.

Well, I shall have considerable trouble in determining the needed parameters. First of all, I shall have to engage in what I have been calling the preselection of intensional descriptions of my options—or, in plainer language, will have to decide how to describe my options. This will be a difficult task, since it will involve balancing against one another such heterogeneous criteria as expense on the one hand and, on the other hand, the gastronomic qualities of the available wines. I mean such things as "sweetness," "aroma," and "smoothness." (I understand that courses for wine connoisseurs teach the identification of no less than eighteen "essential qualities" of wine.) So let us suppose that I don't pretend to be a knowledgeable wine-fancier and am content to rely, as a mere layman, upon what at the time in question I do actually prefer.

But how am I to determine that? Or, to put the question in another way, what will the computer be measuring in a fashion analogous to a thermometer's measurement of heat? Commonsense would be inclined to say: the strength of my desires. The trouble with that is that I am liable not to know what I really want to do until I have made my choice. The orthodox Bayesian view, committed as it is to an operational definition of the elusive notion of "preference" requires me, however, to determine the outcome of a number of hypothetical choices, taking the form of "I *would* take bottle A rather than B" and "I *would* exchange bottle C for a gamble at such-and-such odds on getting either A or B." This is an exacting task because it requires me to imagine a whole series of hypothetical choices subjunctively formulated. And what I *think* I would choose in "pairwise" choices might well differ from what I *would* actually do.

I imagine that a devotee of Bayesian methodology would retort that my difficulties are factitious. Problems of application, I imagine him saying, are to be expected when one tries to be scientific. The complexity of the preliminary calculations needed to determine the direction of radio signals to a space shuttle do not impugn the correctness of the background physical theory. Well, my retort to that defense would be that the really hard work of being a Bayesian chooser is already effectively accomplished once I have obtained the postulated numerical parameters. For the rest, I don't need a computer to choose the largest number.

Apparent Violations of the Model

A more serious difficulty is that conscientious reflection upon my momentary desires and their relative orderings and strengths might well reveal *violations* of the Bayesian choice axioms.

Consider the following hypothetical case: in choosing a secretary from three applicants, I might use the three criteria of, say, expertise, intelligence, and "congeniality," all regarded as equally important. I might then discover that I grade applicant A 3, 2, and 1 respectively (roughly equivalent to "first-rate," "good," and "acceptable"), while B's corresponding scores are 1, 3, and 2, and C gets the ratings, 2, 1, and 3. If I further consider a deficiency of two points in any one category as sufficiently significant to merit disqualification, while differences of one point are too unreliable to disqualify, I shall find that I prefer A to B (for decisive superiority in expertise), B to C (for decisive superiority in congeniality), and C to A (for decisive superiority in intelligence). This kind of circularity prevents application of the Bayesian schema.

If it arose in real life, I would be reluctant to concede that there was nothing better to do than accept defeat. I might want to try at least some of the following ways to make a satisfactory choice: (1) by reconsidering the criteria of "expertise," "congeniality," and "intelligence" in the hope of ranking them in order of importance; (2) get more information by further interviews or additional tests; (3) simply to toss a coin; (4) retain some modicum of decisive choice by tossing a coin to eliminate only one applicant; (5) get a "second opinion" by asking a trusted colleague to advise me; (6) ask the applicants how *they* would like the difficulty to be resolved (a somewhat Solomonic procedure); or (7) even more problematically, apply "affirmative action" by choosing a black or female applicant. But even the "cunning of reason" might fail. To take no action then would, of course, be to behave as stupidly as Buridan's celebrated ass.

Was I being *inconsistent* in my first rankings of the three secretarial applicants? Well, if my conclusions were to be "I *should* choose A rather than B, and B rather than C, and C rather than A," I could infer that I *should* and *should not* appoint A (and also B and C!). That would be a plain case of logical contradiction. But a more accurate description would be, "Considered on their relative merits, I would prefer A to B, B to C, and C to A." That is an accurate account of my feelings at the time. There is no logical inconsistency yet, but what might be called colloquially, having a divided mind. One thing I ought not to do is to treat such a situation as showing that I am *indifferent* to the three applicants. I am *not* indifferent to them in the way in which I would be if I had three applicants whom I regarded as having equal qualifications. It is, in my judgment, more sensible to recognize my dilemma and try to resolve it in some of the ways I have suggested than to press the applicants forthwith into the mold of a weak ordering. The Bayesian approach extols so-called consistency (which really means submission to a Bayesian weak ordering) at the cost of realism and usefulness.

If I had the time, I would want to discuss some other important ways in which the Bayesian axioms fail to conform to problems of decision in real life, paying special attention to the emergence of so-called lexicographical orders of real-life preferences and, even more important, to the severe problems of determining what "preference" and the associated notion of a "utility function" can be taken to mean. But I shall have to be satisfied by ending with some brief remarks about the crucial notion of rationality.

The Elusiveness of Rationality

The notion of rational choice, which specifies the overarching objective of Bayesian choice, is a highly contentious one. Some years ago I distributed a questionnaire designed for those who would consider themselves "educated" (say, those who would be embarrassed to have to confess that they had never heard of Chomsky or Wittgenstein). The results showed an extraordinary amount of disagreement about the correct application of "rational" and "irrational": whether, for instance, backing a horse to win and also to lose (at the same odds) should count as rational, irrational, or neither. Now people without pretensions to scholarship or professional expertise—the overwhelming majority of our fellow human beings—have very little use for the labels of "rational" and "irrational." But they often evaluate choices and decisions, praising them as reasonable, sensible, or thoughtful, or criticizing them as hasty, short-sighted, or foolish. They (and we!) denounce outrageously poor or perverse choices as idiotic, absurd, or insane. These common adjectives seem to me more useful than the pretentious appellations of "rational" and "irrational," which, after two thousand years of learned wrangling, remain so ill-defined as to be hardly worth using.

I suggest therefore that we might do well to declare a moratorium on these contentious and ill-defined epithets and to speak instead of reasonable, sensible, and *intelligent* choices.

We might also do well to think of praiseworthy choice as the exercise of a practical art, rather than the application of a mathematical calculus. If my own view is heading in the right direction, skillful practitioners of the art of choosing well will be good at thoughtful, imaginative, and resourceful consideration of options, will attend to long-term consequences as well as to momentary desires and preferences, and will be sensitive also to aspect-variation and to the distorting influences of prejudice, self-deception, and unreasonable passion. Since prolonged indecision is not enjoyable, the ultimate aim of such informal choice making will be the development of good habits that will allow skillful choosers to act, for the most part, as spontaneously as good pianists. This is an exacting but realistic program. Improvement in choosing and deciding is not easy—but no harder than learning to do better in such difficult arts as medical diagnosis, public speaking, or playing chess.

How useful is Bayesian theory for intelligent choice and decision? Not very, I fear. Its methodology seems to me so shaky that I have to view the case for possession of an admirable choice "machine" as, in the Scottish legal phrase, "not [yet] proven." Meanwhile, one merit of Bayesian theory, in my opinion, is to have unintentionally provided an instructive and cautionary instance of the number fetishism that is so characteristic of our era.

# 8

## *Some Questions about Bayesian Decision Theory*

Bayesian decision theory (BDT) is usually presented nowadays in the form of (1) an uninterpreted axiom system (plausibly regarded as a mathematical "model," representation, or blueprint) containing undefined constants (parameters), together with (2) a less formal "interpretation" of those parameters, expressed for the most part in nontechnical layman's language. If the interpreted axioms are then regarded as empirical assertions, the resulting BDT is a fragment of a scientific theory of free human action.

I assume familiarity with such careful formulations of a BDT as are to be found, for instance, in John C. Harsanyi's writings.[1] In what follows I shall mainly consider choices made "with certainty," by a single person, say Eligo.

Although current BDTs, resulting from nearly four decades of intensive study by mathematicians, economists, psychologists, and philosophers, have been sufficiently impressive to be acclaimed as "among the jewels of intellectual accomplishment in our time,"[2] I believe that the fundamental concepts employed in

---

Reprinted, by permission of Kluwer Academic Publishers, from *Recent Developments in the Foundations of Utility and Risk Theory*, ed. L. Daboni et al., pp. 57–66. Copyright © 1986 by D. Reidel Publishing Company.

1. See, for example, John C. Harsanyi, *Rational Behavior and Bargaining Equilibrium in Games and Social Situations* (Cambridge, 1977), esp. ch. 3.

2. H. A. Simon, *Reason in Human Affairs* (Stanford, 1978), p. 3.

## Some Questions about Bayesian Decision Theory

applying contemporary BDTs deserve the further critical scrutiny that the following, necessarily brief, reflections may perhaps promote.

### Descriptive or Normative?

The pioneers of BDT have characteristically regarded themselves as *scientists*, seeking mathematical models to represent in idealized and simplified fashion the actual behavior of rational decision makers. But since choices and decisions (I shall not distinguish between them in this essay) are prime instances of *free* actions by persons who might have chosen otherwise had they wished, a "science" of human choice will necessarily have normative implications. Thus the familiar admonition of Bayesian theorists to "maximise expected utility" is part of what might be called a Bayesian code (BC) addressed to those who wish to behave rationally when making decisions.

My chief question will be how far the Bayesian code deserves to be respected. More specifically: I wish to consider whether anybody who fails to conform to the BC in some respects deserves to be reprimanded for inconsistency or defective rationality.

### A Simple Illustration

Let us suppose that Eligo, having won a prize in a bookseller's promotion lottery, arrives in the store to choose one of a given set of books. I imagine him to compare them two at a time (pairwise), rejecting each time the one he less prefers. For simplicity I assume for the present: (1) that no ties arise, i.e., cases in which Eligo has no relative preference for either of the two books compared (indifference); and (2) no cases of indecision in which Eligo is unable to make a pairwise rejection. The BC admonishes him to take as his prize the ultimate survivor in this selective procedure.

In this kind of case, BDT postulates that the binary relation of "preference" (call it $P$) shall be transitive (i.e., that if Eligo accepts $xPy$ ["I prefer $x$ to $y$"] and $yPz$, he is always committed to accept-

*153*

ing $xPz$, not $zPx$). If Eligo's behavior violates this condition, so-called cycles will result, such as $xPy$ and $yPz$ and $zPx$ (a triadic cycle). The emergence of such cycles (or those containing more than three terms—having larger diameters as it were) is held to convict Eligo of inconsistency or irrationality.

Qualms about the Transitivity of Preference

Most advocates of BDT consider the requirement of transitivity (and hence the absence of preference cycles) as self-evident. But is it really so? If "I prefer $B_1$ to $B_2$" were to mean something like "I would be happier to get $B_1$ rather than $B_2$," transitivity of the preference relation might well seem as obvious as the transitivity of, say, the relation of "being more expensive than." But contemporary Bayesians, committed to a behavioristic methodology, distrust any subjective expressions of present inclination or anticipated satisfaction. Accordingly, they interpret "I prefer $B_1$ to $B_2$" to mean: "If I were now offered a choice between $B_1$ and $B_2$ alone, I would take the first." Let us call this preferential pairwise choice (PPC).

It is not obvious that Eligo's PPCs, thus construed, will in fact be transitive. For he is being viewed as making counterfactual predictions whose behavioristic verifications would be actual choices between just two books, in situations differing from his actual situation. And even if those many counterfactual predictions were indeed all true, there is nothing in the nature of preference, thus defined, that guarantees transitivity and the consequent emergence of a unique linear ordering.

Eligo might not notice the cycles possibly lurking in the pairwise choice procedure I have postulated. If he thinks that he would reject $b$ in favor of $a$ ($aPb$) and $a$ in favor $c$ ($cPa$), he will be discarding both $b$ and $a$ and so will have no occasion to compare $b$ and $c$. Yet if such a comparison would have yielded $bPc$, Eligo would have been faced with a triadic cycle. (Such unnoticed cycles might well arise in long chains of pairwise choices.)

In general, it is easily seen that the identity of a survivor of a cyclic set of pairwise choices will depend upon the order in which the pairwise comparisons are made. Thus Eligo might, in our example, be committed to *cPa* by one calculation and to *aPc* by another. To safeguard himself against this kind of possibility, Eligo ought theoretically to repeat the entire chain of hypothetical pairwise choices, examining all the pairs of available books in all possible sequences. Even if that yielded no cycles, there would always remain the disturbing possibility that the linear order he obtains might only be part of a large cycle including books not actually at his disposal.

Thus unless the preference relation is transitive a priori, a very conscientious user of BDT in the envisaged situation would have to discover whether his PPCs did in fact yield a unique linear ordering. This would require him to consider PPCs not only between the books actually available to him, but also between them and other books that might have been offered. For one added book might produce a "cycle" that included all the books actually available and thus render the Bayesian injunction to maximize utility impossible to apply. This fantastically elaborate procedure must be viewed as a reductio ad absurdum of any methodology that requires it.

Questioning the Transitivity Requirement

Let us take another look at the alleged transitivity of preference. When completeness (*xPy* or *yPx* for all *x* and *y*) holds for the relation of strong preference between three alternatives, *a*, *b*, and *c*, it can seem self-evident that *aPb* and *bPc* together necessarily imply *aPc*.

For if not, and completeness holds for the pair *a* and *c*, we could derive *cPa*, which, taken with *bPc* would yield *bPa*, conflicting with the assumption that *aPb*. Still more obvious at first sight seems to be the inconsistency of supposing that Eligo might be led to assert *aPa* (as following from *aPb* and *bPa*).

There is no a priori reason, however, why a given binary relation should in general fail to produce cyclicity. An instructive example can be drawn from the so-called pecking behavior of domestic or wild birds. We are told that when a number of hens

*Choice Theory*

are kept in the same enclosure they arrange themselves in a unique linear order, at whose head is an unpecked pecker, while at its foot there is a wretched bird that is, as it were, a pecked unpecker, pecked by all the others. But if corresponding observations are made on a group of three birds belonging to different species, say a hen, a pheasant, and a duck, circularity may result, with hen pecking pheasant, pheasant pecking duck, and duck pecking hen.[3]

The following is a more directly relevant example. Suppose we have three football teams, say Leeds, Manchester, and Newcastle, in which each can be expected to beat the next, on account of, say, decisively superior attack, defense, or stamina, respectively. Their strengths might then be represented in the following diagram (with higher marks indicating higher strengths):

|  | Attack | Defense | Stamina |
|---|---|---|---|
| L(eeds) | 3 | 2 | 1 |
| M(anchester) | 1 | 3 | 2 |
| N(ewcastle) | 2 | 1 | 3 |

I will now assume that the two-point superiority of $L$ over $M$ in attack is sufficiently decisive to outweigh the lesser inferiority of the former to the latter in the categories of defense and stamina; and similarly for the other two cases.

Given such a possible situation, it would not be absurd or self-contradictory to claim that $L$ is overall a stronger team than $M$; likewise, $M$ over $N$ and $N$ over $L$. (The paradoxical flavor of such assertions results from the tug of the comparative form of the expression "stron*ger* team than.")

If one were now offered bets on the outcomes of all the three possible matches between the teams in question, it would be quite rational to bet on $L$ against $M$, $M$ against $N$, and $N$ against $L$. For no "Dutch Book" could be made against such a triplet of bets.

It might be objected that the imagined situation arises only because football teams play against one opponent at a time, while

---

3. For further examples, see M. Gardner, *Scientific American* 231, 4 (October 1974), pp. 120–25.

choices in general may and should be considered in groups of three or some higher number. What would a rational bettor do, it may be asked, if he had similarly cyclical information about three racehorses in pairwise contests and was then considering a race in which all three were running together for the first time? Well, of course, one horse would win, if dead heats were excluded. But the rational response would surely be to have, on the evidence available, as yet no definitive preference. (Here again the breakdown of transitivity is of decisive importance for rational choice.)

It is instructive in this connection to examine Amartya Sen's interesting attempt to show that transitivity is already guaranteed by the assumed asymmetry of the preference relation (the inadmissibility of $xPy$ and $yPx$).

In his inaugural address Sen assumes the correctness of the so-called weak axiom of revealed preference, to the effect that if somebody "chooses $x$ when $y$ is available, then he will not choose $y$ in a situation in which $x$ is obtainable." Sen's derivation of the transitivity axiom (here slightly modified to convert his argument into a direct rather than an indirect one) runs as follows: Suppose that the chooser prefers $x$ to $y$ when offered a choice between just these two options by themselves. Now let him be offered a choice between the same $x$ and $y$, in the presence of a new option, $z$, to which $y$ is preferred. So we have $xPy$ and $yPz$ and wish to show that $xPz$ must hold. As between $x$ and $y$, the chooser will prefer $x$, by our first assumption, so he will not choose $y$; and as between $y$ and $z$ he prefers $y$, by our second assumption, so he will not choose $z$; hence he will choose neither $y$ nor $z$, but rather $x$. Thus, in the presence of $z$, he chooses $x$ over $z$, so his behavior will conform to $xPz$, QED.[4]

Two assumptions are at work in this argument: the first being that possible incomparability between the extreme terms, $x$ and $z$, needs no attention, the second that the addition of further options to the original pair $x$ and $y$ will not upset the previously established preference between them (sometimes called the principle of independence of irrelevant alternatives). I hope to have

---

4. A. Simon, "Behavior and the Concept of Preference," *Economica* 40 (1973), pp. 241–59.

said enough previously to have made the first assumption seem doubtful. And as for the second assumption, I refer the reader back to my discussion of the case of the three racehorses which beat one another in dual contests, while the outcome of a race between all three is indeterminate, to show that this assumption, too, however plausible it may seem at first sight, need not be regarded as having universal validity. For the insertion of new options may well induce a shift of relevant criteria of preference, as previously explained. Hence, Sen's argument for the derivability of transitivity, though of interest to those theorists who will not seriously entertain incomparability (failure of completeness), cannot be accepted in the present context.

## Questioning Preferential Asymmetry

BDT axioms claim that the preference judgment $xPy$ is incompatible with $yPx$, unless some change of preference occurs. This, apparently the least vulnerable of the Bayesian axioms, is open to some objections similar to those I have already raised. For it may well occur in real life that somebody prefers $x$ to $y$ for one good reason and yet also prefers $y$ to $x$ for another good reason. I may at a given moment genuinely prefer to travel to London by car because that would take less time, but also prefer to go by train because that would be safer. So we have here a case, once more, of incomparability or indeterminacy.

To be sure, if we understand by preference only what is implied by actually choosing, then $xPy$ will necessarily exclude $yPx$: I cannot at the same time go to London by car and also go by train. But if we were to take preference in this implausibly behavioristic fashion, we should have to conclude in quite realistic cases, such as that of the choice between car and train, that we could not know what our preferences were until we had acted. We should be like the legendary person who replied to the admonition to "think before you speak" by saying, "How do I know what I think until I hear what I say?" A rigidly behavioristic approach to decision theory would play havoc with the use of the Bayesian system as a normative guide to decisions not yet implemented.

*Some Questions about Bayesian Decision Theory*

Ambiguities of Inconsistency

When proponents of BDT claim that violations of the axioms in the actual behavior of a would-be rational decision maker generate inconsistency, they usually mean logical contradiction. (Hence the tendency to think of a BDT as articulating a *logic* of decision.) Whether one agrees will depend upon the sense attached to the slippery term "prefers." In ordinary life, an assertion of the form $xPy$ is naturally construed as roughly equivalent to something like "I am now *inclined* to chose $x$ rather than $y$," which is not yet a logical contradictory of "I am now inclined also to choose $y$ rather than $x$." And neither assertion is logically incompatible with "But I fancy I shall in the end do something quite different!" Similar remarks apply to such lurking implications as "I think that $x$ might well be more worthwhile" (or desirable, sensible, or commendable, etc.). Any committed behaviorist who wants to reject such statements as unverifiable assertions of intent might well be asked to consider whether his own preferred interpretation of $xPy$ as a prediction (as I assumed earlier on for the sake of argument) must not itself be viewed as an unverifiable assertion of the speaker's or thinker's *attitude*. For there is, as it were, a logical gap between any expression of inclination, desire, choice-worthiness, and the like, and the final decision.

There is a tendency for committed Bayesians to view any departure from what I have called the Bayesian code, that is, conformity with the interpreted mathematical model in order to maximize expected utility, as a manifestation of inconsistency, or, even more damagingly, as a case of defective rationality. Let us consider the kind of deviation that may arise.

Imagine Eligo, in the book-prize example, to have arranged the set of books available in a single order of preference, construed as "present inclination" (but without having used the preposterously "conscientious" examination of all possible pairs to eliminate any lurking cycles). Let $B_1$ be at the head of the list. When the moment comes to announce his decision, however, he actually chooses $B_2$. Has he behaved irrationally? Well, that depends upon his motivation. He might simply have found, at the mo-

## Choice Theory

ment of action, that he then, after all, wanted $B_2$ rather than $B_1$. Or he might suddenly have remembered that he already possessed a copy of $B_1$! Or he might suddenly have recalled previous occasions in which conscientious behavior like a good Bayesian resulted in choices that he later regretted, his attitude being expressible as "It pays to behave like a good Bayesian—and then to trust last-minute impulse!" Or he might wish to show his independence as a free agent, by frustrating the prediction made by an officious friend who had been privy to his calculations. (Such reasons would be all the more attractive if Eligo thought that the calculated advantage of $B_1$ over $B_2$ was slight.) In short, one can imagine any number of sensible reasons for what might at first look like a perverse choice. Would Eligo, in any of these imagined cases, be acting irrationally? I think not.

An accusation of irrationality would be most plausible if Eligo were to explain his apparently perverse action by saying, "I thought $B_1$ was the right book to choose—and *that's why* I didn't choose it!" But even that posture might be defensible. The great and unjustly neglected nineteenth-century writer, Samuel Butler, although a principled atheist, made a point of going to church occasionally, in order not to behave with rigid uniformity. The implied metaprinciple strikes me as eminently laudable and rational. (Whether the reader will agree must depend upon his or her interpretation of that "essentially contested" concept of rationality.)

### Coping with Cyclicity

A confirmed Bayesian, unshaken, as I would suspect, by the difficulties raised above, might well challenge me to offer some promising alternative. I would agree that it is too easy merely to claim that it is more rational (or reasonable, or intelligent) to take the emergence of cyclicity seriously than to brush it aside as evidence of the decision maker's irrationality. How then, should one deal with such cases of indeterminacy?

Consider the following situation: In search of a new secretary, I have reduced the field of applicants to three persons, whose scores on the relevant criteria (say, accuracy, reliability, and skill in human relations) show the same kind of pattern as in the case of the football teams considered above. There are a number of strategies I might pursue to resolve the indeterminacy. For instance: (1) To invoke some extra criterion (perhaps relative need for employment?) which might yield a decisive choice; or (2) toss a coin; or (3) toss a coin only to eliminate one of the candidates, thus leaving me with a modicum of choice; or (4) invite the applicants themselves to make suggestions; or (5) show the dossiers to a respected colleague for an extra opinion; or (6) yield to impulse, hoping that my unconscious motivation may serve better than further cogitation; and so forth. Of course, the problem posed may really be insoluble, but the "cunning of reason" should not be underestimated.

Concluding Remarks

I hope I have said enough to have made a good case for further reconsideration of the alleged usefulness of current versions of the Bayesian code. Had space and time permitted, I could have strengthened this contention by considering the more complex cases of choice under risk or uncertainty. I would like to have discussed in detail the sorely neglected point, familiar to philosophers but mostly ignored by decision theorists, that the options available in serious decision making are necessarily expressed in intensional (with an *s*) descriptions, and the complexities arising from unconscious or deliberate adoption of favored *aspects* of the available options. I hope to discuss these and related matters elsewhere, before long.

# APPLICATIONS

# 9

## On Demystifying Space

I have been asked to open this general discussion by providing a "critique et synthèse" of the papers we have had the pleasure of hearing during these *Entretiens*.[1] Unfortunately, I cannot do so. Such carefully elaborated papers as those by Professors Belaval and Rescher on Leibniz's views about space, or Professor Lorenzen's "constructivist" approach to the foundation of geometry, or the theories of physical space outlined in different ways by Professors Bunge and Törnebohm—to recall only these—cannot be appropriately evaluated without detailed study. When published, the diverse contributions of these *Entretiens* to the illumination of many difficult and unresolved problems connected with space will no doubt evoke the detailed criticism that they deserve. As for synthesis of so many differing and often mutually incompatible standpoints, that would require some super-Hegelian dialectic, powerful enough to overcome (*aufheben*) the prima facie oppositions between far more than two "theses" at a time.

Reprinted by permission from *L'Espace/Space*, ed. M. Svilar and A. Mercier (Bern, 1978).

1. Having failed to understand that I would be expected to deliver a full-length address at the concluding session, I could only improvise a talk based upon notes made during the sessions. It seemed best, in reconstructing the talk from memory, to avoid introducing new matter, confining references and illustrative quotations to the footnotes. I hope the reader will make allowances for the peculiar circumstances of composition.

*Applications*

A knowledgeable hearer of our proceedings might perhaps be struck by a relative paucity of sharply formulated *questions*. I recall the dying words attributed to Gertrude Stein: "What is the answer?"—followed, after a pause, by "But then what is the question?" The challenge remains. The Institut might perhaps consider establishing a commission charged with formulating a syllabus of important and unanswered questions in the philosophy of space or space-time.

Professor Brunner's opening remarks about the topicality of a colloquium on space, in view of the public interest aroused by our newly achieved capacity for space travel, suggested to me a related task. Philosophers have always been expected to improve the "climate of opinion" that is, perhaps optimistically, supposed to be the common property of the educated—in this case, the congeries of views, beliefs, convictions, assumptions, and sheer prejudices about space that are held by our contemporaries. (Though, to be sure, the social and political implications of ideas about space are relatively innocuous, however confused they may be.) Some of our most illustrious predecessors, from Socrates to Hume, have thought it an obligation to attack prevailing superstitions and myths. The philosopher's role as *demystifier* continues to have crucial importance in our own time, when every kind of irrationalism and obfuscation clamors for acceptance and influence.

As my own contribution to this concluding session, I shall outline what a project for the demystification of space might involve.

A useful starting point would be a description of what, with acknowledgments to G. E. Moore, might be called "the commonsense view of space"—a survey of the beliefs about space, and the implicated systems of concepts that are part of the cognitive equipment of any normal adult. A philosopher's armchair is an unsatisfactory place to construct such a conspectus: the resulting list of beliefs and analyzed concepts runs the risk of reflecting what a single sophisticated philosopher thinks that the relatively unsophisticated persons in the street ought to think about space. The relevant empirical facts about laymen's spatial conceptions might better be established by adapting the techniques that our distinguished fellow-member, Jean Piaget, used so brilliantly in exploring children's views about space and geometry.[2] If Piaget could astonish us by his revelations of children's ideas about space, perhaps a parallel investigation of their elders' developed spatial repertories might also surprise and enlighten us?

The data to be yielded by such investigations might be classified as follows:

1. A set of assertions about space, to be distinguished by the reporter as either supposedly "matters of fact" (empirical beliefs) or supposedly "obvious" and "self-evident" (necessary statements).
2. A syntactico-semantic map[3] of the explicitly or implicitly spatial concepts implicated in such assertions, separated into at least the following subclasses: (a) *predicates* (of position, shape, size, orientation, etc.); (b) *relations* (touching, surrounding, containing, above, below, besides, at a distance from, etc.); (c) terms with spatial implications, notably *action terms* (pushing, moving, reaching for, approaching, dividing, breaking, carrying, polishing, melting, etc.).

From such data, appropriately arranged, interrelated and ordered, we might hope to distill some protogeometries,[4] deviating, perhaps strikingly, from the fully developed geometries studied by mathematicians and physicists. Within any such protogeometry, it would be useful to distinguish the strongly held, "obvious" beliefs (e.g., that a circle must have an outside as well as an inside) from the shakier beliefs, arising from the projection of observable features of accessible spatial regions onto the whole of space (e.g., that exactly one parallel to a given line can be drawn through a given point!). (*Do* laymen regard the parallel axiom as obviously true—or are they perhaps only remembering what they were taught in school?) Many of the beliefs thus uncovered, but perhaps especially the "shakier" ones, can be readily made to generate philosophical puzzles.

2. See especially J. Piaget and B. Inhelder, *The Child's Conception of Space* (London, 1956); also Piaget et al., *The Child's Conception of Geometry*, trans. E. A. Lunzer (New York, 1960).

3. I use this as shorthand for an effort to delineate both the syntactical and the semantical rules governing the key words and their cognates.

4. Or "proto-spatiology," if that were not so ugly a neologism.

*Applications*

Let us consider how such puzzles might arise in connection with the familiar notion of an "empty place" or a "gap" between bodies. The "man in the street" has, of course, often seen one body (say this glass of water on the table before me) separated from another (this other glass) by a gap or space. He will nowadays agree that two such objects, if placed in a vacuum chamber, might still be separated from one another (no matter what Descartes thought) and would then have literally *nothing* between them.

Imagine now the following dialogue: "Would there really be nothing between the glasses?" "Yes." "But they don't touch?" "Yes." "Well, how can that be, if there is nothing at all, really *nothing*, between them?" "I suppose there is a *space* between them—otherwise they would touch." "So there is, after all, *something* between the glasses?" "If you say so."[5] The interlocutor is being induced to say that there is nothing and yet also something between the glasses—or even, more absurdly, that the "nothing" in question *is* still "something." The resulting perplexity might be intensified by reminding the respondent that the space between the objects can be *changed*—by moving the glasses—and asking how "nothing" can change or, indeed, have any properties at all. By which time he is likely to be anxious to change the subject and go away to play backgammon or some modern substitute for that game.

How is one to conceive of an empty space or of that aggregate of spaces that we call Space—that nothing that seems also to be a something? One popular and historically influential answer, which has been mentioned several times in our discussions, is the so-called container view of space. The archetypal situation,

---

5. Cf. Descartes: "It may be asked what would happen if God removed all the body contained in a vessel, and allowed no other body to come and take the place of what was removed. The answer must be that in that case the sides of the vessel would *ipso facto* be in contact; for when there is nothing between two bodies, they must necessarily touch each other. It is manifestly contradictory for them to be apart, or to have a distance between them, while at the same time the distance is nothing; for any distance is an aspect (*modus*) of extension, and thus cannot exist without an extended substance" (*Principles of Philosophy*, pt. 2, sec. 18, quoted from the Anscombe-Geach translation of his *Philosophical Writings*, [London, 1954]).

which renders this view plausible, is the familiar one of an empty jar or other container—or of empty seats in some theater. In such cases the empty place is readily conceived as something held open for a prospective occupant and delimited by the bounding surfaces of the surrounding body. A further step, possibly influenced by Aristotle,[6] is to identify the (empty) place with the bounding surface.

When this familiar picture is stretched to apply to the whole of space, the archetype generates a conception of some supreme "container," an enormous room, as it were, within which the drama of the universe is performed. (I think, in this connection, of a sign announcing *"ein Korb voll Neuigkeiten,"* a basket full of novelties, that I saw displayed the other day in a shop near to the congress hotel.)

I have never been able to understand why the "container" view should have been found so appealing as a way of mastering and overcoming the paradoxes that cluster around the notion of empty space. I once heard of a child who found it puzzling that radio could arrange for an aria sung in Paris to be heard as far off as Berne. His father explained it in this way: "You know that if you step on a cat's tail here, the miaow will emerge over *there*. Well, imagine an enormous cat, with its tail in Paris and its mouth in Berne: that's how it is with radio—only there's no cat!" Quite so. An imaginary cat explains nothing; and a nonexistent container leaves us just as puzzled as we were at the start. The container view invites us to think of the whole of space as the interior of an enormous surrounding container (an enormous room without walls)—only there's no such container! If, per impossibile, there were such a thing, our initial puzzles would only be exacerbated. For would not the container itself be in space? And would that not require a further container? And if not, then space itself is not the interior of a "container" (has no bounding surfaces to delimit it). The supposed explanation is a hoax. Strip it of its adventitious imagery that trades upon our familiarity with jars, baskets, and

---

6. Thus: "[P]lace necessarily is . . . the boundary of the containing body at which it is in contact with the contained body" (Aristotle, *Physics*, bk. 4.4, 212a) and "[T]he innermost motionless boundary of what contains is place" (ibid.), quoted in W. D. Ross, ed., *The Student's Oxford Aristotle* (Oxford, 1942), vol. 2.

*Applications*

other receptacles, and we are left with no more than the notion of the largest of all spaces. The initial mystery, if there is one, of how there can be an empty space between material objects is certainly not to be dispelled by invoking the notion of an all-encompassing space that is not bounded by material bodies.

Leaving the container view to the ignominy it deserves, let us now consider its chief competitor, stubbornly advocated by Descartes and by many others since—the theory that conceives of space as a substance.[7] Stated crudely, the view is that what we loosely call empty space is in fact a stuff having only such *geometrical* properties as shape, size, length, breadth, and height ("extension").[8] The dominant imagery here is of a ghostly kind of stuff, later to be endowed with physical as well as merely geometrical properties and christened "ether," that entirely fills the whole of space.[9] Thus, philosophical discomfort at the notion of genuinely empty space is to be relieved by filling it with an etherial stuff. Unsurprisingly, such a "space stuff" or "ether" very soon exhibits paradoxical or downright contradictory features. The most permeable of all substances, offering no resistance to entry, it is yet so rigid and cohesive that it can in no fashion be divided, transported, or destroyed. (Think of some enterprising

---

7. See, for instance, Graham Nerlich's provocative book *The Shape of Space* (Cambridge, 1976) in which he argues elaborately for the contention "that space can and does figure as a real thing in our picture of the world even at the most sophisticated level" (p. 140). Nerlich conceives of space as a "particular" (p. 268 and passim) having an indispensable explanatory function in theories of the physical world.

8. Cf. Descartes: "The impossibility of a vacuum in the philosophical sense—a place in which there is absolutely no substance—is obvious from the fact that the extension of a space or intrinsic place is in no way different from the extension of a body. For the extension of a body in length, breadth and depth justifies us in concluding that it is a substance, since it is wholly contradictory that there should be extension that is the extension of nothing; and we must draw the same conclusion about the supposedly empty space—viz. that since there is extension there, there must necessarily be substance as well" (*Principles of Philosophy*, pt. 2, sec. 16, p. 105).

9. Lord Kelvin held that space is filled with "real matter" in the form of "luminiferous ether" whose properties are better known in some ways than those of "any other kind of matter." He found it necessary to ascribe to it incompressibility, but also an "absolutely yielding character." See the passage from his *Baltimore Lectures* (London, 1904) quoted in my *Models and Metaphors* (Ithaca, N.Y., 1962), p. 228.

entrepreneur offering to sell vacuum bottles of genuine Berne space, advertised as bottled at the place of origin—but, alas, incapable of export and, like land, to be enjoyed only in Berne itself.) The more seriously we take the fiction of space substance, the more paradoxes it generates. The reason is not far to seek: if you propose to explain away some puzzling features of all entities of a certain kind by postulating the existence of a special entity of the same kind, the explanans is bound to have peculiar features absent in normal entities of the kind in question. (An elephant supporting the earth will either be the peculiar kind of elephant that needs no support—or will need further elephants ad infinitum.) If the absence of matter is to be conceived as the presence of a special kind of *matter*, the initial category mistake will be irreparable.

Berkeley, in a famous criticism of his contemporaries' conception of an infinitesimal,[10] referred to "the ghost of a departed quantity." Spaces, when conceived as substances, might be regarded as no better than the ghosts of absent bodies. And Space, with a capital S, would be the greatest ghost of them all.

Bergson severely condemned the tendency, not yet overcome, to spatialize time: there is an equally powerful tendency to materialize space—a special case of the temptations of reification. One might speculate why space lends itself so seductively to such reification: is the rich complexity of spatial concepts responsible—or our necessary acquaintance with matter and space—or something else? (A closely related question is why space seems so eligible as a ground for philosophical metaphors—as in the early Wittgenstein's deployment of "logical space" in the *Tractatus*.)

As prophylaxis against the temptation to reify space, it might be worthwhile to consider how a notion of space might be introduced into a description of chess.[11] Think of the positions occur-

---

10. "A Defense of Free-thinking in Mathematics" (1735), in A. C. Fraser, *The Works of George Berkeley* (Oxford, 1901), 3:63–100.

11. This was suggested by Leibniz's example of the genealogical tree: "[A]s the mind can fancy to itself an order made up of genealogical lines, whose bigness would consist only in the number of generations, wherein every person would have his place.... And yet those genealogical places, lines, and spaces though they should express real truth, would only be ideal things" (H. G. Alexander, ed.,

Applications

ring in some actual game of chess as corresponding to material bodies: count a transition from one such "chess body" to another, produced by the player having the move, as a "motion"; and let the "distance" between any two positions be measured by the least number of moves that *would* be needed to transform one into the other. We can then conceive of an analogue to empty spaces. For suppose a sequence of four moves in the actual game resulted in a position that *could* have, but in fact was not, reached in two moves. In such a case we might plausibly think of the initial position and the fifth (after the four moves) as separated by an "empty" interval of two moves. That interval, one might say, is filled (if one wants to speak in this fashion) by *possible moves*, those permitted by the rules of chess that were not actually made in the game in question. Finally, the whole of "chess space" might be conceived as the ordered aggregate of such "possible" situations. Here, there is little temptation to think of "chess space" as a substance: "chess space" is merely a convenient *façon de parler* for speaking succinctly about what the rules of chess permit.

In somewhat similar fashion, it might well prove feasible to exhibit space as a logical construction out of certain primitive spatial relations between material bodies.

For the sake of illustration, let us confine ourselves to a drastically simplified space of one dimension, partly occupied by fixed bodies (say rigid metal bars) each of them an integral number of centimeters in length. Take as the basic undefined relation between any two of these bodies, that of "touching" (postulated as symmetrical and intransitive, etc.). Then we can easily define a notion of *interposition*, such that a body interposes between two other bodies when it is in contact with both. Two bodies then count as separated when something could interpose between them. We might introduce notions of distance by postulating a class of unitary *measuring bodies* (forming an equivalence class). Thus a body might be said to be at a distance of two units, say, from another when exactly two such measuring bodies

---

*The Leibniz-Clarke Correspondence* [Manchester, 1956], pp. 70–71). Leibniz's use of this example is adversely criticized by Nerlich, *Shape of Space*, pp. 24–28.

*could* be interposed.¹² This kind of program looks feasible, in spite of the severe technical problems that would arise in developing it for three-dimensional space or four-dimensional space-time.¹³

One feature of the proposed construction deserves to be especially emphasized. A crucial step is bound to be the introduction of a *modal operator* in the course of defining and measuring distance and volume: such techniques need cause no concern, now that we have reasonably satisfactory modal logics at our disposal. Assuming this to be permissible, we might reasonably be led to think of space in general as a *permanent possibility of material co-presence;* and talk about space itself would then be regarded as a succinct style for referring to the relations that obtain between actual material bodies and the further relations that *would* obtain if certain specifiable bodies existed.

Such a program is, in my opinion, well worth pursuing because, if successful, it would yield the demystification of space that I desiderate. It is not a program of reduction in some pejorative sense. To claim, as seems plausible, that space is a logical construction out of relations between material bodies does not deny the existence of space in any ordinary sense of existence. I leave the ontological implications of such a program for the discussion that my necessarily sketchy remarks may, as I hope, provoke.

12. I omit here the symbolism, formulas, and illustrative figures used in the original talk.
13. How such problems might be overcome is at least partially indicated in such pioneering efforts as A. A. Robb, *Geometry of Time and Space* (Cambridge, 1936).

# 10

## *The Radical Ambiguity of a Poem*

Some Versions of Ambiguity

*Introduction*

Many literary works, among them some of the most interesting, display *radical ambiguity,* in a sense of that expression to be defined later. I shall argue that even the best-qualified readers may have to accept irreconcilable and conflicting interpretations. I shall also contend that such indeterminacy is not necessarily a bad thing.

The view I shall be opposing can be illustrated by the following quotations. Professor Beardsley says: "If two presentations of the same aesthetic object have incompatible characteristics, at least one of them is illusory."[1] Professor Hirsch says:

> Reproducibility is a quality of verbal meaning that makes interpretation possible: if meaning were not reproducible, it could not be actualized by someone else and therefore could not be understood or interpreted. Determinacy, on the other hand, is a quality of meaning required in order that there be something to reproduce. Determinacy is a necessary attribute of any sharable meaning, since

---

Reprinted, by permission of Kluwer Academic Publishers, from *Syntheses* 59 (1984), pp. 89–107. Copyright © 1986 by D. Reidel Publishing Company.

1. Monroe C. Beardsley, *Aesthetics* (New York, 1958), p. 48. The quoted statement is the last of a set of seven "postulates of criticism" allegedly presupposed by many critics. Beardsley regards the quoted postulate as "stronger than the others and perhaps more debatable" (p. 48).

an indeterminacy cannot be shared: if a meaning were indeterminate, it would have no boundaries, no self-identity, and therefore could have no identity with a meaning entertained by someone else.[2]

To be sure, Hirsch proceeds to say that "determinacy does not mean definiteness or precision," and holds that "most verbal meanings are imprecise and ambiguous, and to call them such is to acknowledge their determinacy." So I am not certain that he holds the view that I am questioning. But whether he does so or not, that view is widespread: many people think that a literary work must have a single "determinate" or "self-identical" meaning, however complex, awaiting discovery by a sufficiently skilled and perceptive reader. Any appearance to the contrary, as Beardsley says, is "illusory" and must be overcome.

Such a postulate of *semantic determinism*, as it might be called, can usefully be compared with the physicist's postulate of *causal* determinism. The triumphs of modern physics would have been impossible unless scientists had firmly believed that behind the flux and confusion of phenomena there are unique causal chains awaiting discovery. Not to have believed this would have been to acquiesce in the disorder of surface appearances, eschewing the immensely difficult work of penetrating to physical reality. Still, physicists have finally been compelled to abandon this belief in causal determinism, in order to arrive at truly comprehensive and adequate physical theories. The situation may be similar with regard to literary studies. Firm belief in semantic determinacy is an insurance against indolent acquiescence in superficial incompatibilities. Yet, a point may come when it is expedient to abandon the belief. I shall rest the case

2. E. D. Hirsch, *Validity in Interpretation* (New Haven, 1967), p. 44. It is not clear what Hirsch is claiming in maintaining that meanings, even ambiguous ones, must be "determinate." When he says that "determinacy, then, first of all means self-identity" (p. 45) he seems to be producing only an empty tautology that places no restrictions upon meaning. But then he proceeds to exclude "an array of *possible* meanings" (ibid.) as inadmissible, on the dubious ground that "the human mind cannot entertain a possible meaning; as soon as the meaning is entertained it is actual." One might think that entertaining a set of possible meanings offers no more difficulty than entertaining a set of possible solutions to a given mathematical problem. Nor does such a feat, *pace* Hirsch, imply "a denial that the text means anything in particular."

*Applications*

against semantic determinism mainly upon a single extended illustration, one of Wordsworth's so-called Lucy poems. But before reaching that point, I want to spend some time in reaching an understanding about terminology.

### *Literary Uses of the Term "Ambiguity"*

Since the appearance in 1930 of William Empson's *Seven Types of Ambiguity*, ambiguity has been almost as popular a notion among literary critics as irony—and has been similarly inflated to the point of uselessness. Empson said: "I propose to use the word in an extended sense, and shall think relevant to my subject any verbal nuance, however slight, which gives room for alternative reactions to the same piece of language."[3] This phrasing was offered by Empson as an improvement on the first edition's formulation of an ambiguity as whatever "adds some nuance to the direct statement of prose." Empson conceded that this "stretches the term 'ambiguity' so far that it becomes almost meaningless."[4] In the preface to the second edition of 1947, Empson says, "I claimed at the start that I would use the term 'ambiguity' to mean anything I liked," and a look at his book will show that he was not overstating his adherence to this Humpty-Dumpty principle. Most of the time, he used the word to refer to complexity or multiplicity of meaning, a topic much broader than anything that I wish to discuss here.

A more recent writer, P. M. Wetherill, in a comprehensive treatise on critical methods, finds ambiguity everywhere in literary texts and notably treats metaphor as exemplifying it.[5]

---

3. William Empson, *Seven Types of Ambiguity*, 2d ed., rev. (London, 1947), p. 1.

4. Ibid., p. 1n.

5. P. M. Wetherill, *The Literary Text: An Examination of Critical Methods* (Berkeley, 1974). "Metaphor is a form of ambiguity" (p. 119). Wetherill concedes that "terms like ambiguity, paradox, irony (and many others) are, of course, pretty crude. A linguistician or a semantics expert could demolish them without too much difficulty. When we talk about the meaning of literature, however, we are dealing with problems much too complex for any scientific linguist to be able to tackle adequately" (p. 119). The complexity of literature might be supposed to be a reason for sharpening one's speculative and analytical instruments, rather than a reason to be satisfied with notions that could be readily "demolished."

In the face of so inflated and ultimately mischievous uses of an important item in the critical vocabulary, one naturally turns for guidance to an unabridged dictionary. The relevant entry from the third edition of Webster's *New International Dictionary* runs as follows: "ambiguity: the condition of admitting two or more meanings, of being understood in more than one way, or of referring to two or more things at the same time." Here we have an amusing example of a definition that iconically exemplifies its own confusion. For certainly the definition does itself "admit of two or more meanings" and can itself be "understood in more than one way" (if those two things are taken to be distinct), and the definition does certainly refer "to two or more things at the same time." It is worth noting, as an example of the confusion that often befuddles our topic, that according to Webster any use of the plural "we" would have to count as an example of ambiguity, since in using the word in this way we do refer to at least two things at the same time.

## Some Paradigm Cases of Ambiguity

Let us then make a fresh start by considering some clear cases of ambiguity, in some suitably restricted sense of that word, and see what analytical conclusions we can draw from them. I am tempted to start with the case of a lecture I heard many years ago, announced by the speaker, a distinguished American philosopher, as "The Nature of Wholes." As I listened to his booming voice, I wondered whether he meant 'wholes' or simple 'holes'—and an hour later I was still wondering. But this example is hardly typical.

Here is a more interesting case. On Friday, April 7, 1775, according to Boswell: "Patriotism having become one of our topicks, Johnson suddenly uttered, in a strong determined tone, an apophthegm, at which many will start: 'Patriotism is the last refuge of a scoundrel.'"[6] "Patriotism is the last refuge of a scoundrel." Are we to take this as an assertion about patriotism—or about scoundrelism—or about both at once? Our answer will

---

6. L. F. Powell, ed., *Boswell's Life of Johnson* (Oxford, 1934), 2:348.

*Applications*

make a difference, since one of these choices will imply something derogatory, perhaps intended half mischievously, about patriotism—and the very existence of the uncertainty produces something of the same effect.

Resort to the context of utterance does not altogether remove the uncertainty. For Boswell goes on to say:

> But let it be considered that he did not mean a real and generous love of our country, but that pretended patriotism which so many, in all ages and countries, have made a cloak for self-interest. I maintain, that certainly all patriots were not scoundrels. Being urged (not by Johnson) to name one exception I mentioned an eminent person whom we all greatly admired.

Thus Boswell seems to have taken patriotism as the logical subject of Johnson's epigram, but we have only his own word for that reading, without any confirmation from Johnson—and only Boswell's own gloss, "a real and generous love of our country." It would not be perverse to say that, in spite of Boswell's exegesis, we are still left in the initial position of having to choose between alternative readings.[7]

Here is another example. Soon after a performance of Pinter's play *The Birthday Party*, a lady wrote to the dramatist the following letter:

> Can you tell me the meaning of your play? There are three points I do not understand. i. Who are the two men? ii. Where did Stanley come from? iii. Were they all supposed to be normal? You will appreciate that without the answers to my questions I cannot understand your play.

This was Pinter's reply:

> Dear Madam, I would be obliged if you could explain to me the meaning of your letter. There are three points which I do not under-

---

7. There is some collateral evidence for Johnson's conception of self-styled patriots, for instance in the second definition of *patriot* included in the 4th ed. of his dictionary (1773): "It is sometimes used for a factious disturber of the government" (cited in the Powell ed., 4:87, n. 2, which also provides some amusing references to the views of Gibbon and Sir Robert Walpole on "patriots.")

## The Radical Ambiguity of a Poem

stand. i. Who are you? ii. Where do you come from? iii. Are you supposed to be normal? You will appreciate that without the answers to these questions I cannot fully understand your letter.[8]

### Comments on These Examples

In the foregoing examples, and in many others that will readily come to mind, it is obvious that the reader or hearer "doesn't know how to take" a given text: there is a genuine hitch in understanding. The basic situation was clearly delineated, long ago, by Sextus Empiricus:

> And in the ordinary affairs of life we see already how people—yes, and even the slave-boys—distinguish ambiguities when they think such distinction is of use. Certainly, if a master who had servants named alike were to bid a boy called, say, "Manes" (supposing this to be the name common to the servants) to be summoned, the slave-boy would ask "Which one"? And if a man who had several different wines were to say to his boy "Pour me out a draught of wine", then too the boy will ask "Which one"? Thus it is the experience of what is useful in each affair that brings about the distinguishing of ambiguities.[9]

Sextus Empiricus put his finger upon the crucial point when he invoked "what is useful in each affair" as a way of coping with ambiguity. But who is to say "what is useful" in the "affair" of reading a poem, a novel, or a play? In the examples used by Sextus, the context of application is familiar and straightforward, involving merely the identification of some person or thing in order to get a command correctly obeyed. But in determining whether uncertainty on the reader's part is to be tolerated in literature, we are embarrassed by lack of clarity about the point of reading fiction or hearing a play.

Ordinary use of the word "ambiguity" in a pejorative sense is supported by an oversimple but appealing conception of the process of communication, explicit in John Locke's discussions of language and implicitly used by many other writers. At one end of

---

8. *New Statesman and Nation*, November 27, 1970.
9. *Outlines of Pyrrhonism*, II, sec. 259, quoted in C. L. Hamblin, *Fallacies* (London, 1970), pp. 96–97.

*Applications*

the communicative chain, according to this picture, we have the supposedly identifiable "meaning" that is intended by the original speaker or writer, and is then expressed or "coded" into a verbal message and transmitted to a receiver, for conversion or "decoding" back into a replica of the original speaker's meaning. (I shall not digress to discuss the weaknesses of this "transmission model," as it might be called.) From this point of view, ambiguity appears to result from looseness or "play" in the machinery of transmission, causing the sender to produce *more* than the uniquely intended message (as when a typist hits two keys at once) so that the receiver gets a message facing in several directions (like a loose signpost that swings in the wind).

Such "hitches in transmission" are not, however, to be confused, as is often done, with such other privative and dyslogistic notions as imprecision, vagueness (in the popular sense of the advertisement "Don't be vague—ask for Haig"), obscurity, or the like. Nor is it to be confused with generality, indefiniteness, or, above all, multiple meaning—"saying more than one thing at the same time." There is no reason to regard a pun as ambiguous in any useful sense of that word—or to suppose that the rich suggestiveness and multiple meanings of an effective metaphor should count as a case of ambiguity. If multiplicity and complexity of meaning were to be deplored as regrettable weaknesses of speech, then the simple sentence "The cat is on the mat" would already have to be criticized for telling us more than one thing at the same time. The inexplicitness of all speech, which is the direct cause of puzzlement about alternative readings, is unavoidable and can only be palliated by adding a supplementary gloss.

*A Working Definition of Subjective Ambiguity*

Let us make a beginning with the following working definition of what I shall call *uncertainty* or subjective ambiguity.

> A text is *uncertain* or *subjectively ambiguous* for a given reader if and only if that reader is unable to decide between two incompatible readings of that text.

Here, I have deliberately stressed the relativity of subjective ambiguity with respect to a given reader, but I shall soon offer a complementary definition that does not depend in this way upon the competence of a particular respondent.

Uncertainty or subjective ambiguity, as so defined, can arise in connection with any feature of a sentence, or a larger text, that has a bearing upon its meaning for a given reader. Thus the causes of uncertainty may be located in grammatical structures (amphiboly), alternative denotations or connotations, varieties of emphasis, and so on. An especially important case is that of uncertainty about the type of speech-act in question—e.g., whether irony or sarcasm are properly to be imputed. For subjective ambiguity to occur, it is sufficient that there shall be some *felt hitch* in the communicative process.

One might be inclined to think, somewhat simplemindedly, that many occurrences of uncertainty or subjective ambiguity simply testify to a given reader's lack of skill, or to some regrettable lack of textual explicitness, which might ideally be removed by asking the author, supposing he were willing, to provide further elucidation.

Years ago, in writing my own commentary on Wittgenstein's *Tractatus*, I wished that I could have asked him to explain the notorious uncertainties, felt by all commentators on that cryptic text, about the meaning of the crucial word *Sachverhalt*. But one might conjecture, in this and other important cases, that the author himself would be unable to remove the uncertainty and would find the enigmatic passages as puzzling as his best readers have done. When G. E. Moore was once shown an early published statement of his, he exclaimed: "Did I say that? How extraordinary! What on earth could I have meant?" Useful though an author's gloss may be, the possibility of subjective ambiguity will always remain, since it arises from the unavoidable inexplicitness of every text. The ideal of "getting everything on the page" is absurd—as even the most punctilious legal draftsmen will agree.

## A Working Definition of Radical Ambiguity

I should now like to shift attention from the notion of subjective ambiguity, or reader's uncertainty, to the notion of the "radical ambiguity" that is my chief concern. I offer a working definition in the following three stages:

*Applications*

A. A text is AMBIGUOUS if and only if it is ambiguous with respect to at least one feature (aspect, dimension, factor, component) of its meaning. [For short: ambiguous with respect to at least one *semantic feature.*]

B. A text is AMBIGUOUS WITH RESPECT TO THE SEMANTIC FEATURE $F$ FOR A GIVEN READER $R$ if and only if that reader is unable to choose between taking $F$ to be $F_1$ or taking it to be $F_2$, where those two readings are incompatible—or would be unable to make the choice if his attention were directed to the need for making it. .

C. A text is RADICALLY AMBIGUOUS if and only if it is ambiguous with respect to at least one semantic feature for *any expert* (sufficiently competent, ideal) reader.

The first two parts of this definition amount to spelling out what I previously called subjective ambiguity. The chief difference from the earlier definition is that I am now allowing for the possibility that a given reader, while not immediately noticing the possibility of alternative readings, would detect a lurking ambiguity, once his attention was directed to an equivocal semantic feature. A controversial aspect of the proposed definition is the transition it incorporates from a "given reader" to an "expert reader," somebody sufficiently competent to satisfy all reasonable demands for reading skill, experience of literature, acquaintance with the particular context, and where appropriate, the style, background, etc., of the author in question.

## The Case of the Slumber Poem

*The Setting*

I shall now report on some readers' reactions to the following poem by Wordsworth.

> A slumber did my spirit seal,
>   I had no human fears:
> She seem'd a thing that could not feel
>   The touch of earthly years.
>
> No motion has she now, no force
>   She neither hears nor sees

*The Radical Ambiguity of a Poem*

Roll'd round in earth's diurnal course
With rocks and stones and trees!

I had better say something first about the occasion. In 1972, my colleague Professor M. H. Abrams, the distinguished literary scholar, joined with me in realizing a project we had long entertained of jointly offering a graduate seminar on philosophy and literature. A largish group of graduate students, a majority of whom were specializing in English,[10] took the seminar.

In order to prepare some materials for discussion, Abrams and I followed the procedure used by I. A. Richards and reported in his book *Practical Criticism*, of giving the seminar members copies of unidentified poems, with instructions to explain in writing what they took to be the poem's meaning. We did not try to specify the instructions further, leaving it to each individual reader to decide how that slippery term "meaning" was to be interpreted. However, we did suggest that the prose paraphrases might be thought of as produced in a teaching situation where the instructor would need to explain "what the poem was all about."

*What the Readers Said about the Poem*

Here is one characteristic "protocol":

[The Poem] centers around a "she" who had been alive, and had seemed to the speaker immortal, who is now dead. . . . We can tell only that she was important enough to the persona for him to speak of her, that association with her caused his "slumber," and that her death affected him in some way. These are the only assertions I can make for certain. On looking closely, I feel the first two lines and the speaker's attitude to her death become ambiguous. We don't know who she is: her influence on the speaker can be read as calming or as malevolent bewitchment. . . . In this case, two different complexes of attitudes towards women are called into play: "she" might be Petrarch's Laura or Merlin's destroyer Nimue. If the meaning placed on "spirit" involves concepts like creative power, inquisitiveness, freedom, then her influence was for the bad: she

10. Ten were specializing in English, two in American literature, four in philosophy, and one apiece in comparative literature, German literature, and theater arts.

*Applications*

sealed him up, stifled him. . . . In any case, she is dead now, and the speaker is awakening from his slumber, relieved, or sad, or both. The second quatrain can then vary in meaning from a satisfied crow to mourning. But there are no emotive words pointing towards either interpretation: we have no hint of which direction to follow.

Another respondent says:

She seems to have been a young girl because she was still untouched by "earthly years" when she died.

Here is another reader who agrees on the identification:

In its barest essence, the lyric is the speaker's reflection on the death of a much esteemed, perhaps beloved female.

These students seem rather confident about the denotation of "She." Others were more cautious:

"She" is an undefined Other: let us presume for now that she was in fact a woman herself.

But later on the same writer says:

We may read the "she" in line 3 as referring to the "spirit" of line 1 (spirits commonly take feminine pronouns).

This somewhat surprising suggestion, that the "she" of lines 3 and 6 is the "spirit" mentioned in the first line, was also favored by several other readers:

His spirit, the "she" of lines 3, 5 and 6 seems to him to have been removed somehow from the realm of ordinary response.

It will be noticed that this reporter (one of the most talented students in the group) takes the identification with the "spirit" as too obvious to need elaboration or defense.

Here are some more in the same vein:

The speaker explains that he felt none of these fears because his spirit no longer seemed to feel that "touch of earthly years."

After the first two expository lines the narrator stops referring to himself directly and centers on his thematic subject, "my spirit" (the only possible antecedent for the pronoun "she" in line 3).

After line 2 the speaker drops "I" and adopts the pronoun "she," personifying spirit. No longer does the speaker identify his whole self or what is happening to him. He discusses instead only what is happening to his sleeping spirit.

I add a few more extracts, to provide some sense of the whole:

'Spirit' initially appears to refer to the speaker's soul or self. Thus, he falls asleep and in sleep becomes immune to fear and the passage of time. Action and perception both cease and he becomes as it were for the time being mindless, like rocks, trees and stones.

The poet is writing about death—his death. Correspondent with the mode of his death—in slumber, effortlessly, without anguish, is his attitude towards his death: calm, dispassionate, like an impartial observer. . . . The closing lines of the poem suggest a picture of the spirit in deepest slumber, like a dormant seed in its remarkable seed pod, oblivious to all physical change; as to whether the seed will ever germinate—only time can tell.

Finally, one sample of some of the wilder flights of imagination:

The first stanza is reminiscent of a situation familiar in ballads: the enchanted human lover and the fairy woman. The speaker is under a spell, his spirit is imprisoned or "sealed," and he does not have normal responses—for example, the fear a human being would naturally feel at an encounter with the supernatural. His enchantress is a female creature, an otherworldly "thing" (untouched by "earthly years").

Some of the writers produced more plausible and very able readings. Nevertheless, I was dismayed at responses such as those that I have reproduced. It seemed astonishing to me that there could be so much honest disagreement about the very reference of the "she" in question.

That the disagreement has serious consequences for the reading

*Applications*

of the poem needs no argument: if one takes the "she" of the first stanza to be identical with the "she" who is "rolled round in earth's diurnal course," the poem's meaning shifts drastically. (For one thing, there is on this interpretation a considerable difficulty in making sense of the line, "She neither hears nor sees" with the implication, I suppose, that the spirit who sealed the poet's slumber had previously been able both to hear and to see.)

## Did the Readers Miss the "Plain Sense" of the Poem?

Astonishment would be a poor word to describe Professor Abrams's reactions to these papers: both he and I were sufficiently astounded to suspect that some members of the class had perpetrated a practical joke. But when it appeared at the next session that the members of the "spirit party" really were in earnest, my colleague tried to show that their reading violated the plain sense of the passage. I remember him arguing that if one took "my spirit" as the grammatical subject of the first line, the implied construction, "My spirit did seal a slumber," violated English grammar. However, the dissenting minority contended, quite plausibly, that poetic license would be a sufficient excuse, if one were needed. At a subsequent meeting, Abrams did manage to shake some of his opponents by giving a detailed account of the circumstances of the poem's composition, its relation to the other so-called Lucy poems, and Wordsworth's placing of it in the first edition of the *Lyrical Ballads*.

At this point in the vigorous debate, I came by chance upon a long and learned essay by Hugh Sykes Davies,[11] an English don at Cambridge University, who argued—possibly with tongue in cheek, but I think not—the very point of view that was taken by the recalcitrant members of our seminar. A good deal of scholarship was deployed in Davies's paper—for instance, in a prolonged discussion as to whether Wordsworth could have referred to something as abstract as "my spirit" by a feminine pronoun.[12]

11. Hugh Sykes Davies, "Another New Poem by Wordsworth," *Essays in Criticism* 15 (1965), pp. 135–61.

12. See ibid., pp. 136–38. Davies's remarkable essay contains, among other good things, what is in effect a small anthology of critics' views about the poem in question.

*The Radical Ambiguity of a Poem*

This unexpected reinforcement rallied the dissenters and left them more than ever convinced that they had hit upon what seemed to them the *correct* reading of this unexpectedly controversial poem.

On the whole, I would judge that the outcome of this long and spirited discussion left matters pretty much as they had been at the outset: Abrams—and I too—regarded the heterodox reading as really rather preposterous; while those who had independently hit upon it resorted to progressively more ingenious epicyclic defenses to objections. (I was reminded of the apocryphal lunatic who maintained that he was dead. When his friends pricked him to show that his blood still flowed, he retorted, "So what? That just shows that dead men can bleed.")

*A Reading by Laura Riding and Robert Graves*

Anybody who thinks that the students' responses might simply be written off as high-spirited and frolicsome perversity might be invited to consider the extraordinary volume of exegesis on this same poem that established writers and literary critics have produced.

In 1928, for instance, Laura Riding and Robert Graves gave the Wordsworth poem some rather rough treatment. They say: "As a prose fancy this poem is confused and illogical; and if it were translated into French it would be no poem at all."[13] Having decided that "the details are even more illogical than the main argument," they accordingly undertake to repair Wordsworth's poor craftsmanship by turning the poem into one that *could* be translated into French. So we get:

"A slumber sealed my *human fears*
  For *her mortality:*
Methought *her spirit* could withstand
  The touch of earthly years.

"Yet now her spirit fails, she is
  Less sentient than a *tree,*

---

13. Laura Riding and Robert Graves, *A Pamphlet against Anthologies* (New York, 1928), p. 128.

*Applications*

> Rolled round in earth's diurnal course
> With rocks and stones and *things*."

This should surely be included in any anthology of bad poetry composed by first-rate poets. Riding and Graves seemed to have felt they could have done better, for they added: "If we could get the rhymes to match the revised sense, this could properly be rated, according to the 'best poem' standard, as a first-class poem."[14] Getting "the rhymes to match" they seem to treat as a trivial matter of technique. (But it should be added that Riding and Graves were using "best poem" sneeringly and thought the poem in question "has great uncanonical beauty.")

### *Cleanth Brooks and F. W. Bateson on the Lucy Poem*

For a more sober disagreement about the meaning of the Lucy poem one might turn to conflicting readings by Cleanth Brooks and F. W. Bateson. The former writes:

> [The poet] attempts to suggest something of the lover's agonized shock at the loved one's present lack of motion—of his response to her utter and horrible inertness . . . part of the effect, of course, resides in the fact that a dead lifelessness is suggested more sharply by an object's being whirled about by something else than by an image of the object in repose. But there are other matters which are at work here: the sense of the girl's falling back into the clutter of things, companioned by things chained like a tree to one particular spot, or by things completely inanimate like rocks and stones. . . . [She] is caught up helplessly into the empty whirl of the earth which measures and makes time. She is touched by and held by earthly time in its most powerful and horrible image.

But Bateson writes:

> The final impression the poem leaves is not of two contrasting moods, but of a single mood mounting to a climax in the pantheistic magnificence of the last two lines. . . . The vague living-Lucy of this poem is opposed to the grander dead-Lucy who has become involved

14. Ibid., p. 129.

in the sublime processes of nature. We put the poem down satisfied, because its last two lines succeed in effecting a reconciliation between the two philosophies or social attitudes. Lucy is actually more alive now that she is dead, because she is now a part of the life of Nature, and not just a human "thing."[15]

I agree with Professor Hirsch, to whom I owe these references, that the Brooks and Bateson readings are in radical conflict. As Hirsch puts it: "No amount of manipulation can reconcile these divergent emphases, since one pattern of emphasis irrevocably excludes other patterns, and since emphasis is always crucial to meaning, the two constructions of meaning rigorously exclude one another."[16]

## Other Readings, Serious and Humorous

If one needs any further evidence, at this stage, of the amount of controversy that this relatively simple poem can generate in the hands of professional critics, I recommend looking at the discussion by A. P. Rossiter. He starts off strongly with a dose of bluff common sense: "If we are concerned with Wordsworth's poems, we must disembarrass our mind of the superfluous fictions generated by editors, and take the poem as Wordsworth offered it—as a single separate lyric on a single 'she' who is dead."[17] But "taking the poem as Wordsworth offered it" immediately reveals for Rossiter yet another ambiguity, connected with "the little word

---

15. Cleanth Brooks, "Irony as a Principle of Structure," in Literary Opinion in America, ed. M. D. Zabel, 2d ed. (New York, 1951), p. 736; F. W. Bateson, English Poetry: A Critical Introduction (London, 1950), pp. 33, 80–81.

16. Hirsch, Validity in Interpretation, p. 229. A little later Hirsch says: "It may be asserted as a general rule that whenever a reader confronts two interpretations which impose different emphases on similar meaning components, at least one of the interpretations must be wrong. They cannot be reconciled" (p. 230). Wordsworth perhaps "ambiguously implies both bitter irony and positive affirmation," but Brooks and Bateson "would be wrong to emphasize one emotion at the expense of the other."

17. A. P. Rossiter, Angel with Horns and Other Shakespeare Lectures, ed. Graham Storey (New York, 1961), p. 48. Rossiter is arguing against conclusions drawn from Wordsworth's varying arrangements of the Lucy poems in successive editions of the Lyrical Ballads (for further details of which Davies's paper can be consulted).

*Applications*

DID." In Rossiter's hands, a concealed ambiguity here produces two more readings, in addition to those already considered, and a conclusion that "the poem is *ambivalent*" (p. 50). And we end with an irenic conclusion, advising us to hold these irreconcilable readings together. "The whole is only fully experienced when both opposites are held and included in a 'two-eyed' view; and all 'one-eyed' simplifications are not only falsifications; they amount to a denial of some part of the mystery of things" (p. 51). I find this policy unappealing.

Finally, for a little comic relief, I recommend the comments of Samuel Butler on another Lucy poem:

> If Lucy was the kind of person not obscurely portrayed in the poem; if Wordsworth had murdered her, either by cutting her throat or smothering her, in concert, perhaps, with his friends Southey and Coleridge; and if he had thus found himself released from an engagement which had become irksome to him, or possibly from the threat of an action for breach of promise, then there is not a syllable in the poem with which he crowns his crime that is not alive with meaning. On any other supposition to the general reader it is unintelligible.[18]

## A Landing Stage

What conclusions are we to draw from this remarkable case? I think that the Lucy poem must be regarded as an irreducible case of radical ambiguity. I see no hope that further study of the poem might resolve the differences between such readers as Brooks and Bateson, or Abrams and Davies, whose competence is unquestioned. For all the relevant information, and much that is irrelevant, is now in full sight. The dispute, indeed, no longer turns on facts. It is, like other cases of controverted interpretation, a matter of deciding *how to take* facts that are in plain view.

---

18. Samuel Butler, *Essays on Life, Art, and Science* (Port Washington, N.Y., 1970), pp. 8–9. Butler says, no doubt with tongue in cheek, "We cannot be too guarded in the interpretations we put upon the words of great poets" (p. 9). His references to the Lucy poems occur in the well-known essay in which he laments the absence from the British Museum Reading Room of the volume of Frost's *Lives of the Eminent Christians* which he was accustomed to use as a sloping desk for his writing.

## On Living with Radical Ambiguity

### The Prevalence of Radical Ambiguity

My chief contention is that some literary texts, such as the Lucy poem, are radically ambiguous. The "best," most competent readers imaginable, possessed of all the skill at reading, wealth of experience, and access to relevant information that might be desired, would be unable to choose between alternative and conflicting readings. The question that a sufficiently informed and perceptive reader might well ask, "Should I take the poem in *this* way or in *that*?" is unanswerable, in the strong sense that there is no conceivable decision-procedure that is applicable. Arbitrarily choosing a reading that one finally prefers is of course not a defensible "procedure," though somebody with an itch for definiteness might do so for want of anything better. I believe this situation to be the rule rather than the exception. We need not invoke such famous cruxes as Henry James's *Turn of the Screw* or Kafka's fictions in order to find illustrations, since the relatively trivial example of Samuel Johnson's remark about patriotism is sufficiently troublesome.

There is, however, little to be said for glorying in ambiguity: the policy of *vive les différences*, indiscriminately applied, is not better than the policy of *cherchez le sens unique, parce qu'il existe*. Indeed, if I had to choose between the two, I would prefer the second, because it encourages, as the other does not, close reading rather than lazy acquiescence in superficial disparities. So let us review some of the plausible ways of eliminating apparent ambiguities (i.e., of showing that they are not "radical" in my sense).

### Eliminating Ambiguities: Taking the Author's Word

When the author is available to settle a dispute between readings, one might think that his verdict would be decisive. But this is not always so. Consider the following instance.

In a poem entitled "1887," published on the occasion of Queen Victoria's Golden Jubilee, A. E. Housman, after recalling the young Englishmen who went to fight and die for the Empire, ends with the words,

*Applications*

> Get you the sons your fathers got,
> And God will save the Queen.

Frank Harris was sufficiently delighted with what he took to be this concluding sarcasm to write to Housman saying, "You have poked fun at the whole thing and made splendid mockery of it." Which elicited the following angry reply:

> I never intended to poke fun, as you call it, at patriotism, and I can find nothing in the sentiment to make mockery of: I meant it sincerely; if Englishmen breed as good men as their fathers, then God will save the Queen. I can only reject and resent your—your truculent praise.[19]

But does this settle the matter? I think not. Harris's "sarcastic" interpretation seems to be an acceptable reading, conflicting with Housman's intentions, but no worse for that. (Unintended meaning is too familiar a phenomenon to need a gloss at this point.)

### The Need to Respect Authorial Reticence

One way in which the author's intention *can* help to reduce an embarrassing plurality of alternative readings arises from the author's undoubted right to leave certain matters unsaid and not even implied—to draw a frame, as it were, around what he chooses to present. How much he chooses to tell is his affair and the temptation to pursue questions of identity, in the spirit of the Baker Street Irregulars, will be resisted by any reader who cares more for the work itself than for playing games that treat the text as a pretext.

A peculiarity of the poetic case is that certain questions that can properly arise in connection with informative communication need to be excluded—and ought not to be pursued further. One might be tempted to ask whether the K. of Kafka's stories lives in Vienna, works in such-and-such a government office, and so on. But the absence of such information might reasonably be regarded as deliberate and as much a part of the fiction as the

---

19. Quoted from Beardsley, *Aesthetics*, pp. 25–26.

spaces in a painting or the pauses in a piece of music. (Of a physical tomato, I can certainly wonder what the unseen back looks like; but surely not in the case of a painted tomato.) Respect for the *author's reticence* and the adoption of a policy of restraint in reading is a commendable way of winnowing the overabundance of plausible readings.

However, one might need to allow for temperamental differences between good readers—between those, like Susan Sontag, who plead for superficial readings and wish to suppress "interpretation" because it interferes with a sensuous response to the work (cf. her conclusion that "in place of a hermeneutics we need an erotics of art") and those, like Empson, who delight in delving for implications and multiple meanings. If so, my conception of radical ambiguity might need to be relativized with respect to such temperamental differences—and so lead us to treat a poem, in effect, as one object for the Sontagites and another for the Empsonites. But this will not dispose of the problem of radical ambiguity, since it amounts to no more than a verbal maneuver.

## Fidelity to the Text

It is all very well to say that the student members of the Cornell seminar treated the Lucy poem as if it were a crossword puzzle or some intercepted cryptogram. There is indeed some justification in treating their overingenious readings as artifacts of the classroom situation. But can we say as much for the opposed readings of professional critics? Certainly one can set aside some of the more fanciful readings of the poem, whether by beginners or expert practitioners, as no better than the willful production of new poems—fantasies on a surprisingly cryptic text of Wordsworth.

We can surely set some restraints upon the freedom of even a good reader to impose any reading that he pleases on the text. In discussing the same poem at a meeting held at the University of Buffalo in 1974, I suggested that at least nobody could reasonably take the "she" of Wordsworth's poem to refer to a favorite *horse*. But some members of the audience demurred, and one proposed that the "she" might be taken to refer to an automobile! (This

*Applications*

would provide a new slant to the concluding image of the poem, with the now permanently stationary car whirled round in Earth's diurnal course.) I don't know how one could argue anybody out of a position as absurd as this one. As well try to demonstrate to the lunatic that he wasn't really dead. One has in the end to rely on qualities of good judgment and good sense which resist formal expression: if someone suffers from semantic blindness, there's nothing finally to do but shrug one's shoulders.

## Is Radical Ambiguity a Bad Thing?

I hope I have at least made plausible my contention that radical ambiguity cannot be ultimately eliminated by recourse to the author's intentions, by respecting the principle of authorial reticence, or by fidelity to the text. We are then left, as I think, with the situation that a given literary work remains for even the best and most scrupulous reader something that can be read in more than one different way.

I should like to insist that the alternative readings remain *in conflict* with one another. This is true even if one takes refuge, as we have seen some of the readers of the Lucy poem doing, in the alleged "ambivalence" of the poet. For the three readings, say $F_1$, $F_2$, and an "ambivalence" between $F_1$ and $F_2$, will remain incompatible if $F_1$ is incompatible with $F_2$. If one feels the need to choose, then I suppose the best policy is one of *charitable interpretation* that selects whichever reading yields the best poem. But what if two of the readings are judged to have approximately the same value?

I would like to suggest that the persistence of incompatible readings is not necessarily a bad thing. (In any case, if I am right, it must be accepted as something unavoidable.) The situation in painting is worth considering, for comparison. I own a painting by Allen Attwell in which a large blue circle, if steadily focused, will disappear. So I have, as it were, two paintings for the price of one. (I should add that this was deliberately arranged by the painter.) More generally, it is possible and, I should suppose, legitimate to view a painting or some other work of visual art from a number of positions, in different lights, and with variable focus of emphasis.

## The Radical Ambiguity of a Poem

There seems to be nothing alarming or uncomfortable about such a variety of perspectival views—nor, I suggest, need the situation be different for literature.

If I am right and interesting works of literary art remain enigmatic and multifaceted as we come to know them better, we shall simply have to accept and exploit such inevitable complexity. Oscar Wilde once said that "truth is rarely pure, and never simple." With the substitution of the word "art" for truth I could agree with him.

# Index

Abrams, M. H., 183, 186, 187
Abstraction, 19–20
Ambiguity
   and authorial reticence, 192–193
   and author's intentions, 191–192
   literary uses of term, 176–177
   paradigm cases of, 177–180
   temperamental differences in readers and, 193
   versions of, 174–182
   *See also* Radical ambiguity
Analogical extension, 8
Analogy, 63–64
Archetype, 8
Aristotle, 100
Articulation of concepts
   ordinary language and, 4–5
   paradigm cases in, 5, 101–102
   respect for common sense in, 6–7
   use-governing criteria and, 5–6
Attestability, 36–37
Austin, J. L., 6, 74n27, 102
Ayer, A. J., 42–43

Bateson, F. W., 188–189
Bayesian decision theory
   consequences and, 135, 137–138
   consistency and, 142–143, 149, 159–160
   decision-making situation in, 133–135
   departures from, as irrational, 153–154, 159–160
   as descriptive vs. normative, 135–138, 153
   equivalence in, 138, 139–140
   features of, 141–143
   mathematical model for, 138–140
   options in, 135, 138, 143–147
   preference relations in, 138, 157–158
   preselection in, 145–147
   problems of application of, 147–148
   rationality and, 97, 101
   self-orientation of choice in, 141
   as synchronic, 141–142
   transitivity axiom in, 153–158
   violations of, 148–150, 153–154, 159–160
Beardsley, Monroe C., 66–68, 69, 174, 175
"Bearer" theory of meaning, 18–19, 20
Behavior, and theories of meaning, 25–26
Bergson, Henri, 171
Berkeley, George, 171
Boswell, James, 177–178
Boyle, R. R., 50, 51
Brooks, Cleanth, 188
Brown, S. J., 71
Butler, Samuel, 190

Carlyle, Thomas, 49
Carnap, Rudolph, 32, 33, 38
Chess
   as case of practical rationality, 106–109
   computer programs for playing, 109n20

*197*

*Index*

Chess (cont.)
  considerations in decisions in, 145
  as model of discourse, 53
  notion of space and, 171–172
Choice, as skill, 150–151
Choice theory. *See* Bayesian decision theory
Classification, definition by, 101
Common good
  E-situation for, 121–122
  participation in commitment to, 128–129
Common sense
  concept articulation and, 6–7
  of metaphor, 78–82
  view of space and, 166–167
Common usage, and technical terms, 100
Communication
  ambiguity and, 179–180, 181
  theory of signs and, 6
Comparison view of metaphor, 87
Concept. *See* Articulation of concepts
Conceptual analysis, and game theory, 116–117
Conceptual field, 104–105
Conceptual innovation, 66
Condorcet, Marquis de, 134
Consistency, 142–143, 149, 159–160
Container view of space, 168–170
Context
  ambiguity and, 178
  linguistic, 41
  of metaphorical statement, 55n11, 88–89
Controversion theory, 68
Conversational implication, 6
Copula, categorical use of, 13n, 79
Creativity, 52–53, 69–74
Credibility, 127–128
Cunningham, R. L., 123

Darwin, Charles, 99
Davidson, Donald, 77–91
Davies, Hugh Sykes, 186–187
Dead metaphor, 56–57
Decision theory. *See* Bayesian decision theory
De Groot, Adriaan D., 107
Descartes, René, 168n5, 170
Desires, management of, 98
Determinacy, 174–175. *See also* Semantic determinism
Dictum, The
  counter-example to, 35–36
  logical status of, 33–34
  neoempiricist embrace of, 30–32
  operational vs. situational reading of, 38–40
  process-product equivocation and, 37–40
  statement of, 30–31
  ungrammaticality of, 31
  user's vs. standard meaning and, 34–35
Distortio, 7
"Doctor's dilemma," 145-146

Emphasis, and metaphor, 57–58
Empiricism, and verificationism, 34, 43
Empson, William, 176
Engram. *See* Physicalistic theory of meaning
Entrapment situations (E-situations)
  with commitment to cooperate, 125–128
  generalized structure of, 118
  indirect approach to, 125–130
  with more than two persons, 121–123
  ordinal structure of, 119–121
  rationality as insufficient for, 123–125
  with two persons, 117–121
"Epi-chess" analogy, 53, 55n12
Equivalence, 138, 139–140
"Ether," 170
Expected utility, 135, 136, 140, 143. *See also* Bayesian decision theory
*Experiment* (magazine), 2
Explication, 33, 90, 116–117
Extended meaning, and metaphor, 84–85, 89

Fact, and reality, 39–40
Fallacy, hidden, 7–8
"'Fido'-Fido theory," 20
Filtering, as metaphor, 47
Frege, Gottlob, 41–42

Gambling, and Bayesian theory, 139
Game theory
  change in rules and, 125–130
  explicative analysis in, 116–117
  logical and mathematical implications in, 114, 115–116
  methodological dogma of, 114
Geach, Peter, 104
General Semanticists, 19

# Index

Goodman, Nelson, 49
Graves, Robert, 187–188
Grice, H. P., 6

Harris, Frank, 192
Held, Virginia, 124
Hidden fallacy, 7–8
Hirsch, E. D., 174–175, 189
Housman, A. E., 191–192
Hume, David, 32

Imagery, theory of meaning and, 21–23
Implicative complex, 59–60
"Indubita," 109
Infinity, 27–28
Instrumental rationality, 97
Interaction, as metaphor, 47
Interaction theory, weakness of, 91
Irony, 89
Irrationality
 choice and, 102, 137, 153–154, 159–160
 departures from Bayesian code and, 153–154, 159–160
 of voting, 122
 See also Prisoner's Dilemma

James, William, 22
Johnson, Samuel, 177–178

Kelvin, Lord, 170$n$9
Khatchadourian, Haig, 71

Language, structure of, 26–27. See also Linguistics
Levi, Isaac, 136
Linguistics
 concept of rationality and, 103–105
 verificationist approach and, 43
Literary text
 as ambiguous, 191
 fidelity to, and ambiguity, 193–194
 use of ambiguity as term in, 176–177
Locke, John, 21, 99, 179
Loewenberg, Ina, 67–68
Logic
 Bayesian choice and, 142–143
 space as construction of, 172–173
 status of The Dictum and, 33–34
Logical Positivism, 31–32
Luce, R. Duncan, 123

Mabbott, J. D., 98

Man-made constructions, 72–74
March, James G., 134–135
Meaning
 linguistic context and, 41
 nonlinguistic consequences of words and, 15–16
 philosophical puzzles about, 15–18
 phonetic differences and, 16–17
 as relational, 28–29
 types of theories of, 18–29
 verificationism and, 30–43
"Mentalistic" theory of meaning, 20
Metaphor
 accomplishments of, 84$n$24, 85–87
 aspects of, 57–58
 as cognitive instrument, 73–74
 common sense of, 78–82
 Davidson's position on, 82–87
 debate on, 48–50
 diagnostic criterion for, 67–69
 emphasis and resonance on, 56–58
 explication of grounds of, 90
 focus of, 57
 as form of ambiguity, 176$n$5
 identification of, 54–56
 interaction view of, 47, 58–60
 literal meaning and, 50–53, 68, 82–84
 operation of implication complex in, 60–62
 other figures of speech and, 49
 projection in, 60
 recognition of, 66–69
 semantics of, 53
 standard meaning and, 88
 substitution view of, 58–59
 truth as, 74–76
Metaphorical thought, 64–66, 78, 81, 86, 91
Metaphor-theme, 54–56
Mind, location of meaning in, 20–24
Models, and metaphors, 62
Moore, G. E., 1, 96, 166, 181
Murry, John Middleton, 48

Names, 17–20
Negation of metaphorical statements, 68
Neo-empiricism, 31–32
Nerlich, Graham, 170$n$7
"No meaning" theory of meaning, 26–29
Nonsense, 29$n$5
Nothing, space as, 168–170
Nowottny, W., 48–49

*Index*

Oakeshott, Michael, 98
Ordinary language, 4–5, 7

Paradigm cases, 5, 101–102
Patriotism, as term, 177–178, 191
Perspective, and man-made constructions, 72–74
Physicalistic theory of meaning, 20–24
Piaget, Jean, 167
Pin-pon puzzle, 16–17
Pinter, Harold, 178–179
Poetry, radical ambiguity in, 182–190
Preference
  aspect-shift and, 146–147
  determination of, 147
  ordering of, 135–136, 138–139
  transitivity of, 139–140, 153–158
Preference cycles, 154–155, 160–161
Principle of Verifiability, 30–43. *See also* Dictum, The
Prisoner's Dilemma
  with commitment to cooperate, 125–128
  general analysis of, 117–123
  paradox of, 113–114
  statement of, 112–113
  *See also* Entrapment situations
Pronominal reference, 182–190

Radical ambiguity, 174
  definition of, 181–182
  elimination of, 191–195
  prevalence of, 192, 194–195
Raiffa, Howard, 123
Rapport, Anatol, 124
Rational choice
  antinomy of, 113–114
  chess playing as case of, 106–109
  elusiveness of, 150–151
  "indubita" in, 109
  moral interests and, 125
  survey on, 150
  *See also* Bayesian decision theory; Entrapment situations
Rationality
  conceptual field for, 105
  as distinctively human faculty, 98–99
  explanations for disagreement on, 100–101
  linguistic approach to, 103–105
  Moore's open question technique and, 96
  Oakeshott's definition of, 98

paradigm case approach to, 101–102
  preliminary definition of, 95–96
  Prisoner's Dilemma paradox and, 112–130
  questionnaire on usage of, 102–103, 109–111
  Russell's definition of, 97–98
  in scholarly usage, 99
  "sociality" and, 124–125
  *See also* Irrationality
Reliable choice, 135
Reproducibility, 174
Resonance, and metaphor, 57–58
Richards, I. A., 2, 58, 183
Riding, Laura, 187
Robinson, Richard, 99
Rochester, Earl of, 99
Rossiter, A. P., 189–190
Russell, Bertrand, 21, 97–98
Ryle, Gilbert, 20, 99

Saussure, Ferdinand de, 20–21, 104
Schick, Frederic, 124–125
Schlick, Moritz, 30, 32, 33–36
Screening, as metaphor, 47
Self-interest. *See* Rational choice
Semantic determinism, 175–176
Semantic field, 104
Sen, Amartya, 157–158
Sextus Empiricus, 179
Shible, Warren, 48
Signs, theory of, 6
Simile, 63–64, 82n23, 86, 87n31
Simon, Herbert A., 134–135
Socrates, 95–96
Sontag, Susan, 193
Space
  common-sense view of, 166–167
  container view of, 168–170
  as a logical construction, 172–173
  as nothing, 168–170
  project for the demystification of, 166–173
  reification of, 171
  as a substance, 170–171
Speech act, 6, 85–87
Speech sounds, 16–17
"Statement-ingredients," 54
Stebbing, Susan, 1
Stein, Gertrude, 166
Stevens, Wallace, 84–85
Strategy, optimal, 106–108
Strong creativity thesis, 70–74
Strong metaphor, 57, 76. *See also* Metaphor
Subjective ambiguity, 180–181, 182

Tolstoy, Leo, 15
Toynbee, Arnold J., 90
Truth, metaphor as, 74–76
Tucker, Albert W., 112*n*1

Uncertainty. *See* Subjective ambiguity
Unintended meaning, 191–192
*Ursprache*, 23
Use-governing criteria, in concept articulation, 5–6
Utility-function, in Bayesian theory, 140

Value judgment, 100–101, 124
Verification, meaning of, 36–37
Verificationism, 30–43. *See also* Dictum, The

Vienna Circle, 43
Voting
  conditional commitment and, 129–130
  as E-situation, 122–123

Weak metaphor, 58
Weak ordering, in Bayesian theory, 138–139
Weil, Simone, 134
Wetherill, P. M., 176
Wittgenstein, Ludwig, 1, 2–3, 30, 38–40, 41–42, 181
Words, 16–17. *See also* Names
Wordsworth, William, 182–190

Library of Congress Cataloging-in-Publication Data

Black, Max, 1909–1988
  Perplexities : rational choice, the prisoner's dilemma, metaphor, poetic ambiguity, and other puzzles / Max Black.
    p.  cm.
  Bibliography: p.
  Includes index.
  ISBN 0-8014-2230-2 (alk. paper)
  1. Philosophy. I. Title.
B29.B542   1990    100—dc20                     89-34777